# Protector

**Dennis Cole**

Copyright © 2024 by Dennis Cole

All rights reserved.

No portion of this book may be reproduced in any form without written permission from the publisher or author, except as permitted by U.S. copyright law.

# Contents

1. prologue — 1
2. |01| — 3
3. |02| — 8
4. |03| — 12
5. |04| — 16
6. |05| — 21
7. |06| — 27
8. |07| — 32
9. |08| — 38
10. |09| — 43
11. |10| — 47
12. |11| — 51
13. |12| — 56
14. |13| — 60
15. |14| — 65

16. |15| 70
17. |16| 75
18. |17| 81
19. |18| 85
20. |19| 91
21. |20| 97
22. epilogue 102

# prologue

It's dark, and quiet. Being alone with my thoughts is tough, but it's the sounds I fear the most.

The sounds mean pain.

Jane is to my left, and she's asleep. I think she does it to avoid the overwhelming sense of despair. It's her defense. I wish I had a defense.

Maybe I do. I don't talk. Not anymore. Not after everything that I've gone though.

There's another girl here, but she's on the other side of Jane, and she's been here almost as long as I have. She's sick, really sick. I never bothered to ask her name.

Why do names matter when we're all doomed? We will all die by the end of this. Slow, long, torturous deaths without mercy.

It terrifies me, but it's reality. Reality keeps me grounded.

There's a scratching sound. I sit up, scuttling back into the corner in an attempt to keep me hidden in the musty shadows. I know what's about to come, and I'm sick to my stomach. Tears start to flow down my face, and I pray it's a short ordeal.

"Look at her, she's terrified!" The words are practically laughed. I whine as the two men stand outside my prison with excited grins.

The barred door swings open with a whine, and I gasp for air. I desperately try to get oxygen into my lungs. It's not working.

I don't beg for mercy. I don't try to stop them.

The only thing I can do is hope that someway, somehow, this will all be over.

# |01|

## Elik

My skin is crawling. Heat rises up my neck, and I stare angrily at the buildings in the valley below me. The sky is dark, only lit by a smear of stars glowing onto the roofs.

There are females down there. Real females.

My kind have no females on our planet. For some years we have scoured the universe for those precious creatures that will bring us companionship, kits. How can we survive without females? It's not possible. It's not right to continue on without finding them.

And we have found them, here on earth.

I've never heard of humans before. None of us have. Aside from Torint. I look over at my comrade who crashed here by chance. He was the first one to find the humans, to take a mate. It's fate that brought us here chasing after him. Apparently, this planet has been through a lot already. There have been wars that killed most of their males.

The females are ripe for the taking.

The few males that are left alive are evil, at least that's what I've heard from Torint. A group of human males stole his mate and tried to torture her. A female. It's preposterous. How can anyone think of harming a precious female?

They are the future. Our destiny.

That's why I'm seething angry. Torint also has information that more females are being held captive in their grasp. They use them for their pleasure, taken without their consent. Such violence and evil should not be taken lightly.

Torint knows this as well, that's why he slaughtered the males that dared steal his mate away from their den.

A mate. That is something I'm still shocked over. Torint is lucky, and he knows it as well. Any of us would do anything to have one of our own.

I look over at Yatik, and then Umner, and finally Torint and Tillip. We're all ready for a fight to rescue the females.

"We approach with caution. We do not know if they have weapons." I inform my team, and we slowly move down the hill in formation. We all are on edge. The thought of a female in danger is not taken lightly.

This mission is essential.

When we get closer to the little buildings that already stink with awful smells, I press my lips together in anger. No female should have to endure this.

We all surround the buildings, curiously searching our surroundings for any sign of life.

"The scent is stale. They must have fled after you killed the others." Notices Umner, and I know his nose is the best. He's right, the male sent is strong, but it's not fresh. It has to be at least a day old.

I try not to growl. They fled like scared little kits.

Tillip rolls his shoulders beside me, shaking his head.

"Let's hope they didn't take the females with them." He whispers, and I want to slap him. That kind of thinking will not help any of us. We must keep our spirits up. I'm too antsy to correct him.

I give the males a signal to move in, a wordless hand signal to go ahead. They follow my order. They burst one of the buildings open, the door crashing down.

It reveals a mess of a living place. This was where they nested. It is disgusting. Making a gruff sound, I shake my head. I'm positive the females are not here, but that doesn't mean we shouldn't search for them just in case.

"Check everywhere. Tillip and I will search the next building." They agree with short nods before entering. I let Tillip follow me as I quickly move on to our next target.

We easily breach the entrance. With a clang, the scent of fear and death assault me, and I choke. It's overpowering. It's horrifying.

I see the cages. The bars of metal in the form of a barbaric box to keep someone in. I pop my jaw. They're here. The females are still here.

Going to the first cage, ripping the barred door right off with one hand. The pure rage that courses through me has no end. I bend to my knees, focusing on the tiny creature in the cage.

"It's alright, female. You can come out now." I whisper, knowing well she cannot understand me. Our language is strange to these humans. They have no translation devices, no way to know what we say. I can only hope my calming tone coaxes her.

She slowly crawls forward.

"Yes, that's it." I encourage her, and I'm shocked when she throws herself into my arms. She's delicate, trembling. Little sobs wrack her chest. Salty tears run down her pretty face, leaving clean trails down her dirt stained cheeks.

I hold her to me, her thin arms wrap around my middle and she sags. She feels perfect in my arms, but I know she is not alright. She needs love and care right now, a gentle hand to guide her and protect her.

I'll be that for her. I know there's nothing that can stop me from accomplishing that. I hold her in my lap as the others find us. Tillip explains what's happened, I hear him mention that one of the humans is dead.

Rage grips me, but I don't let the soft female in my arms see it. Pathetic males, murdering helpless females. There is no honor in it.

Umner tears open another cage, freeing the only other living female. His jaw is set fiercely. He is as angry as the rest of us.

"You are free, female." He insists, and he can't keep the harshness out of his voice. The tiny thing in my hold shivers, crying softly into my chest.

The other female doesn't come out. Umner holds out his hand, trying to show she is in no danger. She remains where she is.

"We are safe. Come out of there." I understand his frustration. She has been locked in this filthy place for too long, and now that she is safe, she still refuses to be free.

But she doesn't know we mean her no harm.

"She cannot understand what you're saying." I remind him. He shrugs, looking disappointed. He eyes the female in my arms, and I clutch her tighter.

I stick my face in her stringy hair. Beneath the stink of body odor and fear, I detect her natural scent. It is sweet and delicate.

Umner expected the female to hop in his lap like this one did for me, and his jealousy is warranted. I am lucky to touch a female. I've never touched one, held one, comforted one.

And now, I have rescued one. She is traumatized, afraid. I know that as long as I'm around, she will never know fear again.

# |02|

------------------------------------------------------

## Penelope

I'm saved.

I can't understand a word this guy says, but he's caused a shift in me I never knew was possible. Whenever the thought of rescue popped into my head, I thought I was hopeless. There's no way I could voluntarily be near a man. And yet here I am.

As soon as the enormous man tore into my cage, and whispered soft, nonsensical words to me, I knew he was here to help. I haven't let go of him since then.

I cling to him, desperate for the comfort he provides. His beard hairs brush my temple. My tears stain his strange clothing. The shirt he wears is barely visible in the dark, but it looks like it's from the future. His language isn't something familiar at all.

But his smell, his deep voice, his hand on my back. It feels like coming home in a strange sort of way. I haven't seen my family in years. We were separated years ago. This stranger, I don't even know him, but he's safe.

I just know that he's safe.

Everything is a blur around me. There's more men like him around the dark shed, but I don't pay attention to them. If I look at them, I'll be overwhelmed. I focus on my man, and listen to his breathing. His heart beat.

As soon as the men that kidnapped us left, I thought I would starve to death. I was going to rot in this cell if it weren't for my rescuer.

"Waytictus marati dur, relinkas." One says, and I stick my face further into my guy's shoulder. He shushes me, his hand cupping the back of my neck. I sob silently.

I'm alive. I'm free. I'm safe.

They keep talking back and forth, but I don't know what they're saying. They're speaking in hushed words. I don't look up, I can't handle it. I hear another cage open. They must be letting Jane go.

"Isa palushins. Ashin olifn rek mista." Someone grumbles insistently. I sniffle, squeezing my eyes shut.

"Abishka ruk delma fashi moeno pal reske." My guy reprimands, his chest rumbling against my body. He holds me tighter, his face going into my hair. I must smell awful.

Of course the men that raped us bathed us, but it wasn't a pleasant experience.

I would always fight when they brought in the bucket of scalding hot water that they poured over each one of us. I still have the burn marks. I shudder at the thought.

This guy is a stark contrast to those men. He's kind, he's gentle. I've never had this feeling before, and I don't want it to go away. He makes me feel safe.

Eventually, the guy tries to stand up, but I protest. I start crying immediately when he tries to help me stand up. I'm a whiny baby, but I don't want him to stop holding me.

No, no, no, no. I say in my mind, grabbing his leg and holding on tight.

"Mucha yestendi jastas?" He asks, and then I guess he realizes I don't understand, and that I won't respond, because he bends down over me. His eyes are beautiful, wide and intelligent, vibrant amber.

His eyes... they're almost... glowing. All of their eyes are glowing.

Who are these guys?

Since he's closer to me now, I reach up, wrapping my arms around his neck so he'll pick me up. He obliges. When he's holding me, he stands up to his full height, and I realize how far up I am off the ground. Wow. He's tall. I look around. They're all ridiculously tall.

What are these guys?

I have no idea, but I don't really care. They're here to save us. Even if they aren't human.

They saved Jane too, but the other girl is dead. She's been dead for days. She died before the monsters left, and they didn't do anything about it. They didn't really care. They left her body to rot.

I didn't know her. I didn't mourn her. At the time, I thought she was lucky to have escaped this. Now I feel awful.

If she held on for just a little bit longer, she could have lived. I feel guilty that I got to survive and she didn't. Now is no time for guilt. I need to have hope.

Sometimes, hope is all you get.

## |03|

------------------------------------------------

### Elik

I'm completely puzzled over the tiny female in my arms. She shudders, even though it's not cold outside, still terrified. She won't let go of me. She's clinging to my clothing, her knuckles turning white.

The tiny thing isn't strong, and she isn't heavy either. I carry her through the woods with long strides. She hasn't made a single sound since we left the awful place she was imprisoned. The other human keeps silent as well, but at least we know that she can speak.

The only thing she's told us is her name. Jane. First Posy, and now Jane? What strange names.

I squeeze the little one in my arms, wondering what she is called, and if she'll ever let me know it.

"She likes you." Tillip comments, walking up beside me from behind. He sways his arms at his side while he walks. I don't miss the fact that he's eyeing my female closely. He's curious. We all are, but I don't like the look he has.

The female won't look up, she has her pretty face pressed into my chest, eyelids closed tight.

I shrug my shoulders, as if it isn't a big deal. The female does like me. She was not happy when I let go of her. She grabbed me and held on tight. I was the only person she wanted.

That appeals to me in a way I can't explain. This little female, this precious creature, she wants me.

It's hard not to relish in it.

"She looks so soft...." Tillip says, reaching one hand out to touch her. As soon as he makes contact with her, she yelps. The human struggles in my arms. It seems like she's trying to climb up my shoulders as sobs rip from her chest.

I step away from Tillip, even as the others turn to stare at the scene. I glare at him.

"Don't touch her." I insist, squeezing my female as I position my body away from him so he can't see her, or try to touch her again.

The tiny thing is trembling in my hold. She clutches at my neck, nuzzling at my shoulder. She trusts me. She knows I'll protect her. I let her calm down, rubbing her back in long motions.

The other human comes closer. Her face is concerned as she studies my female. Jane is making sure that her companion is alright. I'm fine with that. My human does not seem to be afraid of other females.

"Penelope, are you ok?" She asks, even knowing that she will not reply. I look down at her. Penelope? Is that my human's name?

"Penelope?" I wonder, and Jane nods. I look at the human in my arms. What a strange name, but a beautiful one all the same. It suits her. Knotted hair and all.

We continue to stride through the darkness of the forest. Torint assures us that it is safe here. There are no threats in these woods, but I do not trust this strange planet. Especially after finding the treasure that is Penelope. I cannot let anything happen to her.

Eventually we make it back to Posy and Torint's den. He knocks on the door and then stands in the grass so his little mate can see that it is him. He gave her the instructions before we left. He is being careful, after the human males kidnapped Posy he was not taking any chances.

I do not blame him. Females are sacred creatures.

They're bodies soft and warm, their hearts full of love, and they're fierce protective nature of what they hold dear. There are many things we have learned about females back home on our planet. One of those things is that an angry female matches no other beast alive.

I look down at Penelope as I carry her into the den. How is it possible for her to outmatch a beast? It does not seem right that someone so small can be so fierce. Maybe they were mistaken in this, or maybe human females are different.

"Oh my goodness. Bring them inside." Posy insists, biting her lip anxiously as we near the kitchen where a nice smell lingers. It is the warm food that she has prepared for our rescued humans.

She's already filling a few bowls full of the runny food that smells appealing. I consider putting Penelope down so she will eat, but before I can, she grips me harder in protest as if detecting my intentions.

Alright, so I suppose she's not going anywhere. I sit down at the counter top, Penelope content to sit in a ball in my lap. I drag the bowl of soup towards us, lifting the spoon to try to feed her. She looks up at me trustingly, and opens her mouth.

That was easier than I thought it would be.

When I hear whispering, I turn to see the others staring at me, particularly Posy and Jane. They wear worried expressions as they talk. Posy turns to the other human and begins talking fervently. Jane nods reluctantly. Her eyes are wide, her mouth slightly parted.

I assume she's explaining our situation. The simple humans didn't know there was life outside their planet. It must be a shock to them.

Giving a glance at the little female in my lap, I raise an eyebrow when she nestles into me. She does not seem affected by our differences. She has accepted me even though she has no idea where I have come from.

"Penelope, right?" Posh asks softly. My human just burrows deeper into me. She makes eye contact with Torint's mate. Penelope is either shy, or she physically cannot speak.

Either way, I don't want her to feel pressured.

"I'm Posy. These men aren't from earth, but they're here to help. They'll protect us at all costs. You have absolutely nothing to be afraid of." I have to admit, even Posy's voice is comforting to me. The females understand. Well, at least two of them do.

And I know that for whatever reason, Penelope trusts me, and I have to hold on to that.

Sorry this took so long! I will try to write as often as I can. Life gets hectic, and I'm getting over the flu right now. Wish me luck.

# |04|

------

## Penelope

With a belly full of warm food, I sigh in contentment as Elik sets me down. I'm not as panicked anymore. Not as clingy, so I don't insist on him holding me, but I'm still a little clingy. I hold onto his hand like a life preserver.

The idea of being left cold and alone terrifies me.

Elik might be strange, and alien, but I don't care. The guy saved my life. I don't want him to leave me. The mere idea sends a shot of panic straight to my stomach, rolling it with nausea.

My heart rate speeds up when Posy hands me a stack of clothes.

"I'm warming up some water if you want to clean up." She offers, and she's very kind, but the idea of being by myself, even to bathe, it's not good. Everything in me rebels against it. I've been alone too long.

I have to swallow the fear when I take the folded fabric and nod silently. Posy grins. Her shiny blonde hair is tucked behind her shoulder. She's beautiful, and I try not to get jealous.

It doesn't much matter how I look, I survived. Beauty doesn't matter when you're locked up. In fact, it's best not to be attractive at all. Beauty gets you attention. Beauty gets you hurt.

As I slowly follow Posy, I look up at Elik. His face is serious, tense. He always seems to be looking around suspiciously. A neat trimmed beard and his short hair make him a little too handsome. I'm attracted to him, and not only because of his looks. I tighten my hold on his hand. Maybe I do want to be beautiful now.

"Let me know if you need anything." There's a big copper tub, and she pours the last pot full of hot water. She nods at Elik before walking out and shutting the door firmly. I turn to him, and he puts the clothes down on the window sill.

We're both silent, which is normal, especially for me. I've found that Elik is pretty quiet. We're a bit similar in that regard.

I would've thought that aliens were impossible. Aliens? It doesn't make sense. But, after the miracle of being saved, aliens don't seem so far fetched anymore.

"Partrusia mes teak luupin." He murmurs, pointing at the door. I furrow my eyebrows, not understanding what he means. He walks to the door, opening it and standing outside expectantly.

Oh, he wants to tell me he'll be right outside. I smile a little bit, nodding my head. He's so thoughtful. I try not to freak out when the door closes, sealing me in. I don't think about how the room is small and enclosed as I slip out of my clothes and lower myself into the tub.

I try to scrub my scalp as quickly as possible. Washing my body, I watch as the scents and smudges of my traumatic past washes away in the water. It's been a long time since I've gotten to clean myself up. Of course, the men that held us would bathe us. But the water was always scalding hot, and it was a humiliating routine.

The soap smells fresh, flowery. I'm generous with the bar. Pretty soon I'm ready to see Elik again, and I don't want to be alone any longer.

I dry off, putting on the soft clothes and fleeing the room. I realize I'm panting. Panic is overtaking me as the seconds tick by, and I need to see him again. I have to make sure he's still here, that he hasn't left me.

He's still there. His serious face stares down at me, that gaze warming me up, calming me down. I reach for his hand automatically. Elik nods in approval before leading me away.

I follow him trustingly. I trail behind him, almost too close to his back. He takes me to a small room with a queen sized bed by the kitchen. It's warm in here, dark and comfortable. I feel relieved.

Elik takes a step towards the bed, lifting a wooden brush from the bedside table. I subconsciously touch my hair. It's long, and it's also a mess of knots. I gulp nervously at the sight. That will probably be painful, but it has to happen eventually.

My alien must see the fear in my eyes, because he reaches out and gently brushes my arm. If it was anyone else, I would've flinched, but there's something different about Elik.

"Hashel dus melekin." He informs me quietly. Even if I can't understand, his voice is so soft and the only thing I need.

He sits down on the covers, reaching for me slowly. I climb onto his lap. He's immediately touching me, carefully taking my hair in his hands and taking his time parting the tangles from each strand.

There's a few moments where the brush gets stuck, or there's a tug here or a snag there, but for the most part it's actually relaxing. The conditioner I used in the tub helped to loosen the wet locks. Elik is patient, and yet diligent in detangling. Every touch is delicate and measured.

It's the first time in a long time that I haven't felt pain at the physical contact of another person. It feels nice. Pleasant. I don't want him to stop.

Eventually, he's done, and he stands up reluctantly. I'm reminded about how freakishly tall he is. He towers over me, and I bite my lip when he tucks a piece of hair behind my ear. I lean into his hand as he cups my face.

He smiles, a tiny little show of affection before backing away.

"Yaminellish exo palashooka." He murmurs, turning towards the door. Terror sparks me into action. I'm grabbing his arm and yanking hard, but he barely registers my attack.

He raises his dark eyebrows down at me, confusion drawn on his handsome face. I reach deep inside myself, finding any ounce of bravery that I can.

"Stay. Please?" I ask desperately, my voice no more than a whisper. It's hardly audible. I haven't spoken in so long, even I'm shocked.

Elik's face dawns in understanding. I blow out a shaky breath, thankful he has some sort of translation device. I wouldn't mind getting my hands on one of those.

I guide him to the bed, climbing under the heavy blanket and watching him follow suite. He lays down beside me. His whole body is a little bit stiff, but I have other plans. I scoot closer until I can wrap my arms around him.

There's no safer place than tucked under his chin. His muscles gradually become relaxed as he sinks into the mattress. He returns my hold, his hands strong around me.

Sleep finds me swiftly, and I welcome it gladly, snuggling into my man like he's a giant teddy bear.

Happy new year everyone! I hope you like the chapter.

Don't be shy! Leave your thoughts in the comments. I would love to hear from you all.

See you later!

# |05|

## Elik

"Don't look at her like that!" I demand, and Umner's mouth falls open. Everyone in the room stares at me with at least a little bit of fear. All except Penelope. Her wide, dark eyes stare up at me with trust and an acceptance of who I am.

I've never had someone look at me like that.

"What are you talking about?" He demands, and Penelope flinches. I growl. I'm still staring at him with fury.

"You looked at her teats. I won't stand for it." I snarl, and Posy shakes her little head as she covers the table with plates and plates of food. She has a garden, and Torint and Tillip have been providing meat from Earth animals they hunt in the woods. I'm glad we have enough to sustain us.

Penelope is skinny, malnourished. She needs to eat as much as possible. It hasn't been going well on that account. She barely picks at her food.

"What is with you guys and calling them teats? Boobies, breasts, take your pick. Anything but that." Posy says, and Torint gives her a feisty grin.

"What is a boobie?" He asks, and I was quietly wondering about that myself. Posy laughs. I suppose we're not getting the answer to that question. I rest my face in Penelope's hair. Her neck smells delectable.

Someone clears their throat, and I grumble when I look up to see who's begging for attention. It's Umner. I glare at him.

"What do you want now?" His eyes widen at my words, and I can feel the rest of the group tense at the sudden outburst. I know what they must think of me. My family has a history of anger problems, and I know they can see it plain as day. What they don't understand is that I would never hurt an innocent person. I won't let history repeat itself.

"I'm sorry. I didn't realize it would bother you. It's hard not to... look at them. They're beautiful."

His description of her body has me bubbling inside. He can't talk about her that way. He can't look at her there. The anger grows to be too much, grabbing my senses in a steel grip. My breath comes out in harsh puffs from my nostrils.

A tentative hand touches my chest over my uniform. I still, my eyes slowly moving down to make sure I'm not imagining Penelope touching me. Her pale face looks worried. She's worried about me.

I pull her closer, knowing she won't speak in front of all of these people. Last night she talked to me. Only me. She hasn't said a single word to anyone else, and that is a sign to be sure. She does trust me. No one has ever trusted me as much as her.

And everything about her calms me. Just looking down at her beautiful face has erased my anger completely. All I can think about is my little human.

"Whatever." I murmur, ignoring everyone except Penelope for the rest of the meal. Time goes by quickly as I hand feed the female snuggled into me. I never thought that this would happen to me. If you told me days ago that I would have a female curled up on my lap eating from my hand, I would not have believed you.

Here she is though, and she's amazing. I shouldn't be too possessive of Penelope. She's not mine. I don't own her. But inside, deep down, I already think of her as my mate.

That's dangerous. Of course, she wants to be near me and I agree to it willingly, but that doesn't mean she wants to become my mate. I can only dream. I won't force her to do anything she's uncomfortable with, she's been through a trauma. I won't expect anything from her besides what we already have.

I watch from afar as Jane and Posy encourage Penelope to help them with the dirty dishes. She looks up at me with a bit of alarm in her eyes, but I nod encouragingly at her. She needs interaction other than myself. She needs friends, and I need to report back to headquarters.

It's important that I log everything that's happened, and inform the Emperor of our findings here on earth.

Being discreet, I sneak out the back of Posy's den. My radio has better reception outside than under a roof that just gets in the way. I stare up at the dark sky and think of Rytaria, my home planet. It's similar in the dreary clouds, but not the sensation of water through the air or the hot environment. I don't find Earth's weather pleasant.

It only takes a few moments before the device in my hand connects. I hold it up to my ear as I survey the tree line.

"Elik! My most trusted General, how is this planet? Is it what Torint said? Females?" The Emperor's voice demands on the other end of the communication device. He does not have much patience.

I nod my head even though he can't see me.

"Yes, we already have three females in our custody."

"Are you taking good care of them? Protecting them?" He asks impatiently, pressing me for information. I'm compliant. All I want is to get this over with so I can get back to Penelope.

"Of course. They are sacred. The future of our race. Torint says that they are breeding compatible, the computers confirm it." I explain quickly. There's a long pause before he speaks again.

"What are they like? Are they glorious? Beautiful?"

I don't even have to think about my answer.

"More amazing than you can imagine."

Before I can say more, I hear my name being called from inside the house. My head swings around to watch two human females rush outside. I barely have time to end my call with our leader.

"I have to go."

"Alright, I am sending several ships to earth. I want you in the air, on your way home as soon as possible. I haven't announced this to the public, but I will as soon as you're back. Don't let me down. I'm trusting you."

He hangs up, and I rush to Posy and Penelope who are already close. I meet them halfway. My human does not look so good, her cheeks are flushed, tears rolling down her face.

I rip her from Posy who has a comforting arm around her shoulder. She comes willingly, clutching at me as she trembles in my hold.

I growl at Posy. Not in a threatening way, but still angry. I can't scare a female, or hurt one, it's disgraceful. Even if I did want to, Torint would not stand for it. He would try to kill me if he thought I was a threat to his mate.

It's been known since the dawn of time that Rytarians are very protective of their mates. Males are known to tear off limbs. It might explain why I'm completely furious.

"What happened?" I question harshly, and Posy won't look away from Penelope, biting her trembling lip.

"I don't know. We were fine until she realized you were gone. I think she's having a panic attack. I didn't know what else to do." Her voice is high pitched, brimming with fear. I see the tears forming in her eyes. Great. Now I'm dealing with two emotional females.

Maybe it's just the fact that they're humans.

"Let's go back to the den, everything will be ok." Posy nods frantically at my suggestion, and I lift Penelope into my arms. She's stopped shaking, but she releases small sniffles as I walk.

I'm desperate to get her alone, away from everyone. That's where she'll be calm.

As soon as we're inside, Torint rushes towards his mate. It's almost as if he sensed her turmoil and is here to save the day. He swiftly wipes her tears away. He's already murmuring soft words to her and cupping her face while he leans down to be closer to her.

I shove down the jealousy that strikes me hard, and I storm away to slip my own human into her bed where she'll be secure. As long as I can show her that she's safe, than I'll be happy. She's all that matters now.

So glad for all the good feedback. I really appreciate you taking the time to vote and comment. Y'all keep me going, get me inspired.

I still don't have a regular update schedule for this story, but I will update as often as I can!

# |06|

## Penelope

I'm on edge when we board the ship. Elik is sure to comfort me, his broad arm is heavy on my shoulder, pretty much trapping me against him. I don't mind it, in fact, I welcome it. It makes me feel grounded.

The others are ahead of us. Posy and Torint are in the lead, and once again I find myself a little jealous of Posy. She's brave where I am not, she takes charge while I stay hidden in the shadows. I can't help but wonder if people would like me better if I were like her. Or Jane. She went through the same thing I did, but she can still talk and act normal.

I stare down at my feet as I walk along the metal ground of the ship. This planet broke me, and I'm leaving for good.

Sayonara.

Not a drop of doubt is left in my mind as the ship rattles to life, ready to take off. There's not a fleeting moment where I question this decision. A planet full of men terrifies me, of course it does, but I'll be with Elik. I take a deep breath. I need to stay calm.

We take a left turn in the enormous ship, separating from the rest of the group. I don't mind, because I trust my alien man. Every now and then we'll pass another huge alien. All of them do the same thing. They stare at me with wide, amazed eyes. It's a bit scary. I look away, and Elik growls something in his language at them.

They scuttle away like they know what's good for them. I can't help the little flutter that burns in my stomach.

Eventually, we end up in a large room filled with equipment. Elik's arm leaves me, and he strides across the room to the shelves stuffed with things of all different shapes and sizes. I clutch myself in a hug to keep warm. He left me cold and empty.

I notice that most everything in here is some type of electronic. Little lights flash, some of them give off a deep hum. The Rytarians have lots of inventive things that we don't have on Earth. Including translation devices.

My heart picks up the pace. Is that what he's doing? Is he going to give me a translation chip?

It doesn't take long for my question to be answered. Elik turns around swiftly, a little black case in his hands. He stares at my ear with a troubled expression. I notice his fingers are trembling. What's got him so riled up?

He opens the tiny container, reaching inside and pulling out a chip. He frowns, pressing his lips together in a harsh line.

I take a few steps forward to meet him in the middle.

"Abachi tok." He murmurs, worry in his eyes. "Yanici." I have no idea what he's saying, but it sounds like an apology. What does he have to apologize for?

One of his hands cups my head, while the other snakes up my ear with the blinking device between his fingers. Once it touches my skin, I moan in pain.

Scorching agony assaults me, and I can't focus on anything else. Then, in a fleeting moment, it's gone. I desperately try to catch my breath as I stare up at Elik's worried face.

"I'm sorry, little female, I knew it would hurt, but it had to be done." He says slowly, his voice a thunder crack in my dim world, "It pained me more than you could know."

He pulls me into his chest, a safe place to remain. I close my eyes, listening to his heart thud roughly against my ear, knowing that this man cares for me. That's a miracle, because he's all I've ever wanted.

Elik is very quick to hustle me out the door and down the hall. I don't know where we're going, but he holds tightly to my hand. His fingers are warm and strong, safely guiding me through unfamiliar terrain.

Eventually, he stops short, a tall metal door in front of us. He uses his other hand to type a long code into the keypad. I don't recognize any of the symbols on the buttons, and I'm shocked anyone could remember a sequence that long.

The door slides open with a ding, and the alien pulls me in with him. When the door closes behind me, I let out a breath I didn't even realize I was holding in. We're alone behind a thick door with a long code. I'm safe here.

Safe from their eyes, and the hushed whispers they share.

I hate having so much attention focused on me. I've learned that attention is not something that I want, because it ends up with me getting hurt. Somehow I know that Elik won't let that happen.

I observe the room. It's not too big, not too small, but cozy all the same. The bed in the middle of the floor takes up most of the area. It's absolutely enormous, the tall headboard against the west wall. I've never seen a bed so big, and I wonder why there would be a need for such a thing. One glance at Elik, and I figure it out pretty quickly.

Rytarians are huge.

"What do you think?" He asks me gently, guiding me under his arm so he can look down at my face. I try to smile, but my lips don't move much.

"It's wonderful." I tell him, glancing at the bed and wanting to snuggle the rest of the night. I think all my worries will disappear in this room, in his embrace.

He shakes his head, a serious look on his handsome face.

"No, about the ship? The translation chip? Is it much different from your Earth?" He presses, and I nod silently. It's very different from Earth. I wasn't very old when the world went insane. I don't remember much, but I know we didn't have advanced spaceships or translation devices.

Elik leads me to the bed, and lifts a bag onto the covers, sifting through the clothing until he pulls out a few things. I glance curiously at the outfit he has picked out. Those aren't sleep clothes. Terror hits me.

"Where are you going?" I wonder in a whisper, sitting cross legged on the bed. He shifts his beautiful eyes up to me.

"We are going to eat in the cafeteria." My belly does a flip flop, and it's not out of hunger.

Elik must sense my distress, or see it painted crisply across my face. He cups my chin.

"What is wrong? Are you not hungry?" Sure, I could use that as my excuse. I nod my head. He grumbles our a grouchy sound. "Well, you will eat regardless. You need food and energy. I will take care of you."

My lungs constrict, and I can hardly breathe. Elik grabs me by the arms.

"What is it, Penelope?" I burst into tears, and he wraps himself around me, the bed moving under his humongous body.

"I don't want to be around Posy and Jane, they probably think I'm some whiny baby. I cry so much." I sniffle, the tears I shed are immediately soaked up by Elik's soft shirt. "And I'm afraid of everything. Everyone. I don't want to be around so many men."

Continuing to cry, I want to be embarrassed of how much crying I'm doing in front of him, but I'm not. He's always comforting me, taking care of me. He doesn't seem to mind.

"They do not. They know you are strong, you survived what many could not." He promises, rubbing my back. I wipe my eyes with my shirt sleeve, wishing I could just stay here wrapped up in his arms all day and all night.

"But you must eat." Elik sighs, and my muscles instinctively tighten at the thought. "Would you like to have our meal in private? I can ask someone to have our food delivered here. Would that ease your worries?" He wonders as he carefully tucks a stray lock of hair behind my ear.

For the first time in a long time, I smile.

Sorry this took so long, I've been a little lazy I guess. I'll try to have another chapter soon! Thanks for sticking around, and being so patient

## |07|

### Elik

I hold tightly to Penelope's tiny hand. Leading her through the ship is scary for her. I can tell she tries to hide it from me, but her eyes are wide and she leans into me. She's not used to others, she doesn't want to be around them, but I haven't been out of our room in 3 days.

As much as I care for the little human, she has to come out eventually, even if it scares her. She feels secure enough around me to agree. I want to see my teammates. I also want to bring Penelope to the healer to make sure she is healthy as can be.

Last night I was kept awake with terrible thoughts of her sitting in that rotting cage. How terrified she must've been. How much pain she felt. I should've found her sooner. I should have been there to kill the males who raped her and beat her.

Now I am worried about diseases that could only make her even more miserable after all she has been through. I will do anything in my power to keep her safe from harm.

I've let the team know that Penelope's appointment will come first, and none of them understood but Torint. He knows how it feels to be caring for a female. I glance down at Penelope. Especially such a tiny one. She's about the same size as Posy.

It is something to get used to, females Rytarians were large and strong. Humans are the opposite. They are frail, and so soft. It feels just right, like it was meant to be that way. It's almost as if their supple bodies and kind spirits are made to ease the burden of a warrior, and the hardened muscles of a male are built to protect and provide for their every desire and need.

That is what I will be for her. Her provider. Her protector,

Penelope's fingers clench and unclench on my hand, she bites her lips nervously as her shoulder continues to brush against my elbow. She glances around cautiously. Every time another male passes, she practically shrinks into me, glancing at the floor. She wants to disappear from their gazes. I know the feeling well.

It is flattering, her want to be near me, and I enjoy her touch and her trust, but I am worried about her ability to function. I don't know what I'm supposed to do to help her be comfortable or normal without me at her side. It makes me concerned with what might happen if we're not together.

We reach the healer, and he beckons us to come inside. He's welcoming, smiling at us. I hold Penelope in front of me, two comforting hands on her shoulders.

I quickly notice that there's another male in the room other than the healer. He stands by the wall, watching us with narrowed eyes. His arms are crossed across his chest. He stands ere as if he is the captain of this ship. I want to growl at him when the human moves her body around until she's behind me. He's making her nervous.

"Why is he here?" I ask, and the healer turns to us with raised eyebrows. He's acting innocent. How dare him let another male around my human? She is absolutely petrified.

"I want to make sure that you do not harm the female." The soldier stalks towards us with curiosity, and intimidation. It is meant to frighten me, but it has the opposite effect.

Penelope whimpers. I snarl.

"Why would I ever hurt her? She is female. She is sacred. I will protect her with my life." I swear, and he keeps coming towards us. I growl out a warning. I don't want to fight him, and if he comes and closer I will.

"I do not want to fight, any violence around her and she is in danger. She's too delicate to survive." I reprimand, and I feel Penelope's little heart beating wildly in her rib cage. I know I am right.

Can't he see how terrified she is?

The healer slips away, disappearing through the door. I growl. He is not much help at all, he was too frightened to stay.

"I can't see why you would care. Your father certainly didn't mind killing females, and I'm sure you're just like him. You look too similar to him to be any different."

Before I can try to throw a fist, Penelope darts away, trying to escape. She's a smart female, she knows how dangerous it can be when two males get into a fight. Unfortunately, the soldier sees her run, and he makes a dive for her.

I yell out in absolute rage when he grabs her around the waist. As soon as he seizes hold of her, she screams and thrashes against him. It's a useless attempt at trying to get free, it's like a kit freeing itself from his Pa. She's much too weak to do anything.

"Calm, female, I am helping you. Everyone knows how evil Elik is. Do you know what his father has done!" He shouts at her, and I'm beyond angry, but too terrified to intervene. What if she gets hurt? I will never forgive myself if I can prevent her harm,

Penelope begins to cry, fainting against the stranger. His eyes grow wide with confusion at her little sobs of protest. He relaxes his hold. Now is my chance.

I rush to them, but not before a storm of soldiers marches through the door, separating me from my human. I push at them, but it's no use. There is a wall of them. They restrain me, 3 of them grabbing my arms and wrenching them behind my back. They do the same to the male who holds Penelope.

That's where the healer went, he went to get backup to intervene. It never ends well when males battle. They are doing their job.

She falls to her knees, collapsing on the ground. She sniffles, and one of the soldiers reaches for her. She manages to stand, stumbling out of his reach and through the door.

"Penelope!" I shout, but she does not come back. Fear pulses through me. She does not know this place, she is just blindly running. I throw back an elbow. It's a direct hit, the male behind me groans and grabs for his bloody nose. Now that I'm free, I burst forward.

I'm barreling down the hallway, shoving everyone out of the way. She can't have gone far. I have to find her. What if she runs into more trouble? Or worse, what if it's me she is running from? I stumble at the idea.

Does she believe that awful male like so many others do?

The story of my Pa has been twisted over the many years. What they say is true, he killed my mother, but it is not that simple. It was not out of malice. It was out of love and mercy. He loved his mate as all males did.

Maybe I can explain that to my female, but I have to find her first.

I run through the corridors, slamming open doors and frantically screaming her name. Everyone I pass stares and openly dodges my oncoming battle. My breath comes in harsh pants as I search for my purpose.

That's what Penelope has given me. Purpose.

Just when I think I won't find her, I enter a quiet corridor that's completely empty. I pause, hands on my thighs as I catch my breath. Frustration builds, and I feel hopeless. That's when I hear it. A sniffle, so insignificant that I almost miss it.

That has to be her.

I move down the hall until I find an alcove, and in the corner sits the human. She glances up at me, her eyes rimmed in red and her legs hugged to her chest. It's the position she takes when she wants to look little. It works. She appears so tiny and fragile.

While I stand above her, I think of what I should do. What if that male's big mouth destroyed her trust in me? What if she doesn't want to be around me anymore out of fear?

My heart squeezes in my chest. I hate the idea, but if she no longer feels safe around me, I will leave her be.

But, amazingly, Penelope stretches out her arms above her head. She's reaching for me, biting her lower lip as a single tear slides down her cheek.

Relief floods me, and I bend down to pick her up under her arms. She wraps around my front, legs winding tight around my waist. Her head nestles my neck, and I hold her there against me.

Finally, I have found what I've always longed for.

Peace.

New cover art, who this? Worked super hard on the art for this story, thought it could use something different, you know?

But seriously, sorry it took so long to update. Life is crazy. Hope you like the chapter!

Let me know what you think

# |08|

## Penelope

I try to stay quiet, biting my fist to keep the loud sobs from overtaking me. The hot steam feels great in my lungs, but it doesn't stop the river of tears and pain.

Elik is right outside the bathroom while I shower, and he's very worried. He has every right to be. I know I scared him. I scared myself.

We were napping in bed, and I woke up from the most horrible dream. I was back in my cage, clutching at the metal bars with dirty hands, and the men were coming to get me. They were going to hurt me like they did so many times before. I called for my brave alien to come help, but no one came. I was alone again. I cried out, and then I was back in bed with Elik.

When I woke, I was covered in sweat and panting like a dog. Elik was frantic. He didn't know what to do to help me, especially since I fought him, because I didn't remember who he was. I kicked and thrashed when I realized he was on top of me. I didn't know what was real and what was fiction. Reality is a tricky thing for me. After all I've been through, I'm having trouble staying upright.

Luckily, I have someone to lean against.

I rigorously scrub my face of any tears, and turn off the hot water. I sniffle, trying to stay quiet. It was hard enough trying to get into the shower alone. Not only am I attached to Elik, but it would seem he is just as enamored with me. He was not very happy that I wanted to get clean after waking up a sweaty mess. It meant being separated when I'm having a nervous brake down.

Despite my sadness, I smile a little. He's so sweet. Too sweet, actually. I don't know what I'd do without him. It's only been a few days since we met, but I'm already falling hard for the big alien man.

That should scare me, but it doesn't. I mean, for all I know this planet will have other plans for me. They could take me away from Elik.

My breath freezes in my lungs at such a terrible thought. It's not too far fetched, that one alien guard tried to steal me from him. I wrap a towel around my body, trying not to let my thoughts get away from me.

No one will take me away from him. I won't allow it, especially since I wouldn't be able to function.

There's not one particular thing that makes me so dependent on Elik, it's absolutely everything about him. His calming voice, his sweet spirit, his protective nature. It makes him Elik. It makes him the best guy in my book. Not to mention, he saved my life. There's still a part of me that is baffled by that.

I quickly dress in the comfortable clothing I've been given. I push my wet hair from my face while I unlock the door. Carefully, reluctantly, I step out into the room, wringing my shirt in my hands.

Of course, Elik is there to greet me, a fact which makes me smile. He's immediately in front of me with his arms wound tight around my shoulders. He clutches my head to his chest with a strong hand.

"I was worried, you were in there too long, little one." He admonishes, and I shrug weakly, gladly nestling into his hold.

"Sorry." I mumble. Elik sighs, shaking his head before leading me to the bed. I sit down on the edge of the mattress. He goes to the com, which I've learned is a phone, and starts pressing buttons. They flash brilliantly in the dim room.

My curiosity peaks, and I bite my lip, a little nervous to ask what he's doing. I shift uneasily, and he hears, because he hears everything. Nothing gets past him. He catches my gaze. He looks angry, but his eyes soften.

"I am calling the healer. We need to go back and make sure you are healthy." He insists, and my eyes widen. My heart rate triples when I remember the terror I felt at that appointment. That guy grabbing me, the officers running in. I had a panic attack.

And I think I'm having one right now.

"Penelope! Human, stop your tears! Please. I beg of you." Elik's tortured face comes into focus. He's right in front of me. He's real. He's here. When he touches me, it's like all the pain leaks away. "Seeing you cry hurts my heart. I cannot stand it."

His words are so tender, and I throw my arms around him. His strong arms wind around me as well, pulling me forward until I can't get any closer. I've never felt so safe. I give a little hiccup from my crying, he chuffs in amusement. That's embarrassing.

"I will be with you the whole time. I will ensure that nothing like that happens ever again. I will kill any male that tries to touch you, but you need to be checked over. I worry for you, my sweet human. Your mind, it is injured, and it must be treated like any injury. You need love and care to ensure that you heal properly." Elik brushes a thumb across my cheek, looking up into my eyes. He sits on his knees in front of me, always knowing what to say. He's so smart. So empathetic.

I sniffle, feeling silly. I look so stupid. So pathetic. I can't even go to the doctors without freaking out? I'm terrible.

"Yeah, I know you're right." I whisper, and he looks glad at the admission. "But, not right now. You're the only medicine I want. I'll go soon though. I promise."

The enormous alien man clenches his jaw before touching my fingers gently. A little grin grows on his face, and I can't help but be proud that I'm the only one who can make him smile.

"For someone so little, you are very stubborn."

I giggle at that. He's not wrong. My parents always told me I was too persistent. That was before, before we were separated. At the reminder of that horrible day, I sober. I try not to cry. I hate being such a crybaby.

"What is the matter?" Elik asks in a soft voice, and I grip his hands for support.

"I was just thinking of my parents, and how much I miss them." I admit, and Elik's dark eyebrows furrow. I reach up and caress his beard. It's a bit coarse, but I love to touch it. The hair is so thick on his jaw.

"I miss mine as well, though I do not remember my mother as much." He tells me, and I can tell that he is reluctant to talk about them. His eyes wander, his neck tensing.

He opens his mouth to say more, but I stop him.

"You don't need to tell me what happened, not until you're ready to share." I say, and I can see how grateful he is.

Elik quickly returns to hugging me. I squeeze him with all my might. He knows how much I need him, but I don't think he realizes that I love him more than anything, and how I wish that he needed me just as much.

Sorry for the short chapter, hopefully they'll get longer as time passes! Next chapter will be up next Wednesday. Have an awesome week! Stay well, stay home, and remember to practice social distancing!

## |09|

### Elik

I would think that being snuggled up tight to the female that I already think of as my mate would be wonderful. And it is very pleasant, but I am not as comfortable as I would like to be. The sensations are too much for me to handle. I am a physically strong male, but she makes me feel weak as a newborn kit.

The lights are off, and Penelope's breathing has not yet even evened out, so I know she is awake. She remains very still in my arms. I ease away from her, my desire to touch her body too strong for me to stay in the same position for long. I will give in if I stay here with her. Then she will hate me.

She wriggles when I scoot back, as if she's annoyed that I would distance myself from her. I smile at the adorable nature of it, but I cannot put her at risk, no matter how much she wishes to torture me.

She has been through trauma. I cannot be selfish since I wish to mate with her. The vision of what she would look like without clothes makes me swallow a growl. I am a monster to be thinking such things when she innocently lays beside me.

Penelope turns under the covers, and even though it's dark, I can see her squinting at me across the large nest. She's wondering why there is so much space between us. I clench my jaw as she follows after me.

This was not the plan, and now I am in trouble.

I roll out of the nest and onto my feet in one swift motion. I stand, looking over to the bed where a very disoriented human female sits up. Her eyes are wide with confusion.

"Elik? What's wrong?" She wonders, leaning over the flick on the wall light above the nest. It's glow is dim and barely highlights her beautiful face.

"Nothing. Do not worry. I have just decided to sleep on the couch." I tell her, grabbing a pillow and trying to slip away, but she does not accept my deception.

"Don't lie. What happened? Did I do something wrong?" Her voice is so sweet, and heartbreaking. It's soft plea of sadness will not stand, not as long as I'm around to ease her worries.

I quickly neal before her, touching her hair and face to reassure her of my dedication to her. She leans into my touch, closing her eyes as she nuzzles my palm.

"No, my dear human. You can never do anything wrong. I swear this." I say with conviction, her eyes open, tears growing already. A shoot of panic grips me.

"Then what's wrong?" She presses, and I smell her pain. She doesn't like me keeping things from her. I sigh. I want to be honest with her, but I don't wish to frighten her. She is easily spooked, and I would hate to be the one to disturb her.

"I feel desire." I say, my voice a low rumble. She tilts her head to the side as if she does not understand. "A desire as a male, to claim you as my mate."

Understanding dawns on her pretty pink face. She shivers, and I close my eyes as pain overtakes me. Of course she wouldn't want me. I knew this would happen, she has been taken against her will. Raped by vile males.

Then why do I feel as if it is personal? Why has it hurt my feelings? Why do I ache?

I get back to my feet, stalking away with my heart hurting. I will sleep away from Penelope if it means protecting her from myself. It is the only way. She is everything to me, she must be kept safe.

"Wait! Come back." She demands, and I turn in shock. She's standing there before me, so tiny yet so mighty. She is so brave when she wraps her arms around my waist. I just told her how I wish to take her and she wants to touch me still? How is it possible?

"But those human males... they touched you.. you are not ready." I assure her, and she nods begrudgingly in agreement. Then her eyes light up with mischief, and I wonder what she is thinking.

"They never kissed me." She says softly, and I nod, bending to kiss her on the head. It was a common exchange between mates before the disease took our woman.

Penelope reacts by giggling. It is my favorite sound, I wish to hear it all day.

"No, silly. On the lips." I raise my eyebrows, my nostrils flaring. Is she serious? Is that something that humans do?

I think back to the only Rytarian human couple that I know, and suddenly remember Posy and Torrent pressing their lips together. A kiss. On the lips. I never thought such a thing existed.

Penelope leads me back to the bed, and I am mindless as I watch her take my hand and drag me behind her. She is small, half my size, but she holds all the power here. Once I am on the nest, she scoots forward, pushing her hair out of the way as she climbs on my lap. I lean back against the wall and she comes after me.

She is doing the pursuing, leaning forward as she grabs my head in her tiny hands, pressing those red lips to mine. They are so soft, and they taste so good.

I am lost in sensation, and my eyes automatically flutter shut. I shift positions, pulling my little female closer to me until she's pressed against my chest. I move my lips, my tongue, my hands. They all roam and flex as I let myself enjoy this new activity that I am slowly realizing is my new favorite thing to do.

Sorry for another short chapter, I promise they will get better! For now, enjoy the first kiss. Finally, right?

Next chapter will be up next week. Not committing to any specific day, because it's hard to know how my week will be.

See you soon!

# |10|

## Penelope

I look at the wide arrangements of different foods. Many of them smell and look very appealing. The only problem is that none of them are familiar to me. I bite the inside of my cheek, chewing on the skin while I watch Elik load his plate with foods of every color. There's piles of things that he's picked out.

Luckily, he doesn't pressure me to get my own plate. He chooses things that he thinks I'll like, solely based on what I've eaten from the meals they've sent to our room. All the decisions stress me out. I'm thankful for his help.

I take Elik's offered hand that he holds out, lacing our fingers together firmly. He leads me through the crowds of men shoved into the small cafeteria. I guess that everyone on board the large ship is in this room at once. It's almost too much, but I hold onto Elik. He's my hope.

He finally convinced me to leave the hidden haven that is our little apartment style room. It's been a week since our first kiss, and we've kissed a few times since then. It's been a blissful time, and I'm kind of scared of what's to come in the future.

We're almost to Rytaria. We could land there any day. Then I'll really be the center of attention. I hate the idea. I look up at Elik. He looks straight ahead as he guides me with a gentle tug. He's so brave, he could face anything. It inspires me to be more like him. Fearless. Strong. I can be that for him, I have to be.

"Hey, Penelope!" An excited voice calls, one that's distinctly feminine, and all too familiar. Jane and Posy sit side by side, elbows brushing. I offer a small wave and smile as we get closer.

Torint has a heavy arm draped over his mate's shoulders. He nods to Elik, and Elik nods back. His other teammates are here too. They light up at the sight of their leader. I grimace a little, knowing it's all my fault that they haven't gotten to see him for the whole trip. He's been so hyper focused on me, and I've selfishly kept him to myself.

Elik slides down onto the bench after me, but what I don't expect is when he scoots me forward. He sits behind me, his powerful thighs on either side of me. I'm trapped in front of him, but I don't mind. I feel safe. I am safe.

"Did you hear the news?" Posy asks with excitement. I shake my head, watching Elik grab for some type of chicken leg thing and taking a ravenous bite that you would expect from a warrior.

"I'm pregnant. We're having a kit!" Her announcement is hardly contained, and Elik's reaction is to choke on his food. My mouth drops open, and Posy smiles happily, actually laughing when Torint gives a boastfully puff of his chest.

"So soon?" Elik asks, and I can't see him, but I sense his shock. "Why haven't you told me?"

"Maybe because you were holed up with a pretty little human female." Muses Umner. Elik growls in a warning, but everyone just laughs. I smile a little. They're just teasing. It's good to have friends to hang out with. He should be happy he has them.

I shyly look up at Posy and Jane through my eyelashes. They laugh and smile, exchanging words as they eat and talk. They make it look so simple. As if socializing is actually fun. I aspire to be like that. Before everything happened to me, I could easily talk with people. It all ended the day I was taken, my mind slowly deteriorating until I thought that there was nothing left of the person I once was.

But slowly, I'm changing, as I figure out that I can heal. Elik is showing me I can be better, that I can grow.

"I'm so glad you're here, Penelope." Jane says, reaching across the table and putting a hand on mine. I glance at her, and she nods at me reassuringly. I resist the urge to pull my hand away. Sometimes it's an automatic reaction to avoid physical contact. But her touch, it's comforting.

I nod, not speaking still. I find that it remains a difficult thing to vocalize my thoughts. Maybe I'll try harder in the future.

Leaning back, I realize how lucky I am to have the man behind me. Except he's not a man, not really. Men are evil, at least most of them, and Rytarian males have honor. They treat us with respect. Elik doesn't make me feel bad about my recovery. He accepts the fact that it takes one step at a time.

I don't have to expand my comfort zone too quickly.

A large hand makes its way into my view, a fork with food floats in front of my face. Elik's warm mouth presses against my ear.

"You must eat, sweet one." He tells me, urging me to take a bite. I oblige him. The flavor is delicious, and I whisper a thank you, not knowing the reaction I would get. They're all staring at me now. Apparently, they weren't expecting me to speak, even if it was fairly quiet.

I ignore them. If I see all those males looking at me, I might freak out. I'm tired of Elik seeing me have panic attacks. I hate seeing him worry, and wondering what he might secretly think of me. Though deep down, I know that he could never think bad of me. He treats me so kindly. He's so gentle, and I never would have expected it from someone of his size and mass.

Looking at Posy and Torint, I wonder if Elik will want to be my mate. The idea seems so intimidating, almost impossible. Would he want me? I know he likes to kiss, but would he commit to a relationship?

I'm not ready for sex. Not after what I've had to live through, the idea is scary. But I have an inclination that it would be different with Elik. Kissing him is amazing. I never dreamed I would want such intimacy for the rest of my life, and yet here I am. I'm almost anxious to get back to our room so we can do it again. Kissing him is the best thing imaginable.

But I see myself being open to the idea of spending the rest of my life with Elik. He hasn't asked me if I want to be his mate. I try not to let it worry me.

We've both changed for each other, and that has to count for something.

100k reads! Thank you so very much! I love each and every one of you, and I'm so thankful for your support.

I will see you soon with a new chapter!

# |11|

## Elik

I hate this, really truly despise it. One minute I'm holding Penelope's hand, and the next I'm being told she has to have a check up before she can even leave the ship.

And they don't want me to go along with her. I glance down at her, and see her apprehension. She does not want to go with this male. He's insistent though. We land soon, very soon. It's urgent that she's looked over before being able to enter society.

"Posy and Jane already had their check ups. It will not take long at all. You will be returned to your mate immediately. This I swear." He directs the soft words at the human. I almost choke, hearing myself referred to as her mate. It's too enticing. I can only dream of something so lucky to happen to me.

Penelope makes no move to correct him. Although, she doesn't speak to anyone save for me.

I place a hand on her shoulder. It only makes sense that they wouldn't let me go with her. Last time we attempted to get her to our doctor, I started a fight, but it was not my fault. I refuse to admit that anyone was at fault besides the guard who struck my temper.

And Penelope ran for her life. If she got lost, or got hurt, it would be very bad. I fear for others lives if my sanity is at risk.

So, it is best that she goes alone. I don't think she is ready, however, even if she has made very good progress. We have eaten many meals at the cafeteria, and she smiles at the other females. She hasn't started to talk to them, but she is glad in their company.

It makes me very happy. She needs friends. She needs to get better. I will do whatever it takes to help my female.

But, to my surprise, Penelope nods her head up at the male with a brave face. She turns to me. I grip her arm with worry. I don't want her to take on too much at once. It might be too much for her to handle.

"You are sure?" I press, and she just nods. I reluctantly let her go, eyeing the guard leading her with a firm glare. He knows not to touch her. He keeps a safe distance between them as he shows her down the hall.

She glances behind her shoulder at me, right before she disappears behind the corner.

I sigh, burying down every urge I have to run after her and protect her from all discomfort. But I can't. This is good for her. She will be safe. A Rytarian would never harm a female. Not to mention, she will get the medical care she needs to make sure that she is healthy and strong.

Hurrying back to our room, I grab our things, which is only two bags. Penelope came with nothing but the clothing on her back and the bruises on her skin. The only things she has are the clothing pieces I've gotten for her.

The ship rattles around me, and I know that it's landed. There aren't many people on this ship, but as they all file towards the hatch, it clogs up the hallways. I hope that Penelope hasn't been let out of the clinic by now. She will be too scared to face an entire crowd of people.

I'm so protective of my little human female. I don't want to be without her, it makes me too anxious. Her touch calms me. Her presence soothes me. I crave her like I crave the air I breathe. I have already become attached to her in these short weeks.

It terrifies me. I am so dependent on a delicate creature, and it's already obvious that some people don't want me to keep her. My father and mother's history is not my ally. Though her death was a mercy, no one sees it that way. Only my team and a few others believe the story, they know what really happened

After finally being freed from the crowded hallway, I stand outside the door of the ship, looking around the planet we've just landed on. My home. I feel a calm spread over me as soon as my feet make contact with the soil. This is where I belong. This is where I'll take care of Penelope. She belongs here too, this is her home as well.

"Elik!" A voice calls out, and I turn to see an old friend approaching me. I haven't seen General Fray in a long while. He looks much the same, broad in the shoulders and having a grin to share with everyone. He's the most powerful and well respected General on the planet.

I am not much for hugging, but he insists on it. He wraps his arms around me and slaps me on the back several times before stepping back to look at me. His silver hair glints in the wind.

"How was Earth? I am going soon. We're being sent soon to go retrieve more females. I assume you've seen one of them?" He presses, excited at the mere idea of one. I do not blame him. We've been taught that they are mysterious creatures that bring blessings and love. Everyone wants one of their own to share their life with, and their kits that they'll make.

I open my mouth to respond when a quiet presence pauses behind me. I turn when a little hand wraps halfway around my arm. Penelope stands beside my elbow, her head leaning against my bicep. Fray gasps, and my female flinches.

"As you can see, I am very well acquainted with a female." I tell him, and he doesn't respond. He just stares at her. "Are you alright? How was the healer's office?"

She hesitantly looks up at me, biting her lower lip. I can tell she wants to speak, but being around the other male prohibits the words from coming out. I put an arm around her frail shoulders, hugging her snuggly to my side in reassurance.

"It was okay. I thought of you the whole time." She tells me, only looking up at me with determination despite her feather soft voice.

I smile, feeling like the luckiest male on this planet to have her think so highly of me.

"I'm very proud of you. You are brave to go alone." I praise her, and she beams up at me from the praise.

Fray clears his throat. I glance back at him, and his face has gone serious. He won't stop staring at Penelope, but I don't feel threatened by the look on his face. He looks at her as she is, a special being capable of miracles instead of an object that he envies.

"I have to get going. Our ship deploys soon. All I do is pray to the Gods that I am as fortunate as you when I reach Earth." He turns his attention back on my female and he smiles. "It was a privilege to be near you. You are a sight that gives us all hope."

With that, he walks away, there are many other ships around on the landing center grounds. There's a bit of bustle as people come and go. One thing remains the same, almost every male stops to stare at Penelope. I need to get her out of here.

"Let's go find Torint and the others. We need to be escorted to the Emperor's palace." I tell her, and she agrees, taking hold of my hand and following me like it's the only thing she wants to do.

Hope you liked the chapter! See you all next week

# |12|

-------------------------------------------

Penelope

    I'm running, but my legs ache. They want to give out so badly. They didn't sign up for this, and neither did I.

Tiny branches slap at me, and shouts and leers echo around me like a painful mantra as they chase me relentlessly. I pant heavily. I'm not in good shape, never have been very athletic, but my life depends on any fitness I can scrounge up. I have to call upon my deepest endurance. I regret never working hard for it when I had the chance.

I can make it. I just have to keep pushing.

My body rebels, my muscles screaming at me to stop. I'm so tired, so very weak. I've barely eaten anything in weeks, it's so hard to find food or a nice place to sleep. I've been alone, but I though I was safe. Clearly, I haven't been as safe as I thought I was. Those things were the least of my worries all along.

I stop for only a moment, leaning on a tree, the sharp bark coarse against my hands and scratching my palms. I use it for support as I catch my breath, but the noise of yelling bouncing around the forest has me moving once more. I'm reluctant to put my faith in any direction, I saw how many men they had with them, this could be a trap.

For some reason, I never thought something like this bad could happen. A little voice in my head tells me I cannot let them get to me, or something bad will happen.

Footsteps shutter behind me, thumping the dirt like heavy bricks as they catch up with me. I scream before I'm even tackled. I go flying along with the heavy body on my back. My face smashes into the unforgiving forest floor, scraping on pebbles and leaves as I'm pushed down.

The man in question puts a firm hand on the back of my head. He shoves me down to keep me from squirming as his labored breathing continues against my ear.

"I got her!" He screams victoriously, followed by howls of excitement as they gather around. I've never seen this many men before, I thought they had almost been wiped out. Why are there so many of them? What do they want with me?

When a knife presses to the delicate skin of my cheek, and I whimper. Tears pour out of my eyes as my heart leaps wildly like I'm a small, trapped animal, which isn't too far off from my situation. I scream when the bastards starts to dig in, terrified that I'm about to die.

"She's a pretty one. I know just what we're going to do with you, cutie." Someone whispers in a hoarse voice. His weight doesn't leave me, but I hear cheers as the tell-tale sound of a belt buckle being undone reaches my ears.

That's when I know that being killed isn't the worst thing they could do to me.

Two large hands take me by the arms, shaking me gently but firmly as a heart wrenching scream pierces the air. My name flies around my head.

"Penelope! Female, wake up! Please." The voice is tortured, brimming with fear as the screams continue.

My eyes fly open, expecting to see the men from my memory standing around me, but it's just Elik. Wonderful, handsome Elik who's cradling me in his big arms as the screams come to a raging halt, and soft sob follows. I guess I was the one screaming, maybe that's why my throat hurts.

I'm still afraid, so afraid of people who can't even hurt me anymore, let alone try. Why do I have to remember every night of my imprisonment? Why do I have a perfect memory of every word, every ounce of hurt, every moment of terror? It's not fair.

I close my eyes as Elik pulls me into his chest, sighing and rubbing the back of my head with his fingers. I clutch at him, worrying that he'll disappear, terrified that it's all one amazing dream that will leave me wrecked.

Those men, they made me feel so worthless, so empty. I don't know if I deserve Elik or not. He's too good to me, too special to want someone as ruined as me. I'm not pure. I'm not clean. I've been touched by dirty hands, forced to endure wicked things.

But Elik doesn't see that, or he doesn't know the full extent of it. He just holds me, murmuring soft words that I don't even hear because I'm too panicked.

What if he found out everything? If he knew, would he dump me with someone else and then leave? Would I ever be able to see him again? I cry harder, lost in my own mind as it tries it's hardest to drown me.

"I wish I could go back to Earth and track down every one of those filthy males so I could rip them apart and bring you their hearts that I tear from their fragile chests." He growls with so much ferocity that I stop crying. As morbid and disgusting as that sounds, I'm blown away that he would do that for me.

He really cares. For some reason, he doesn't think that I'm worthless and broken. He actually wants me to be happy. I sniffle against his chest. My eyes close, my limbs stretch before curling up into a ball.

Elik is so warm, and I let myself get comfortable. I could lay here for the rest of my life and be content, I just hope that he'll let me.

A surprise chapter, because I think we all deserve a pick me up right about now :)

Next chapter will be on Wednesday

# |13|

-----------------------------------------------------

## Elik

The Emperor's board of supervisors is hard to get into. They rarely speak with someone as lowley as me. I'm so unimportant compared to them. I've never been in their room or meetings before. It's strange to be standing before them and their hungry eyes. The ceiling is tall, the white pillars glistening. It's a magnificent place to be. I don't feel as though I belong here.

As the only General that landed on Earth, and having saved a few females, I am commanded to attend this meeting alone to discuss the planet and what all transpired while we were there. I was informed that the Emperor will not be attending. He's too busy announcing to the whole city that we have a female human, and that she is pregnant with a Rytarian baby.

It's a true miracle. I knew before Posy told us that humans and Rytarians are compatible to create kits. It's a whole different thing hearing that it worked, and so quickly too. Who knows how long Posy and Torint mated to create the kit, but it wasn't long.

Once I'm standing before the board, they look me up and down. 5 males, all of them with their attention focused on me.

Penelope is with Jane, and I'm thankful she trusts her enough to be without me. They connect on a special level, because they went through that awful tragedy together. I hope she will heal a bit more while I am away.

"So, you have brought back only 3 females?" One of the members asks, finally starting the conversation even though I've been here for several seconds, just standing in silence.

"Yes, we were told that there are plenty more on Earth, but we were ordered to come back home."

One raises a hand, his eyes focusing on a computer tab on the table. He has a look of concern as everyone turns their attention onto him.

"Is it true that Torint decided to kill several human males?" My jaw clenches at the mere mention of the males that hurt my Penelope. I don't like to think about them, it makes me too angry. I often remember them when Penelope shows her signs of trauma. She has nightmares, and still feels uncomfortable around too many males. I try to cover up my fury when those side effects of abuse make themself obvious, but I can't help but think of all the ways I could slaughter them.

I wish I could have been the one to end them instead of Torint, but he got lucky opportunity. I would have loved to make them bleed.

"Yes, that is correct. They were abusing females, kidnapping them and hurting them." The board's reaction is what I expect, they're shocked. A few gasps, widened eyes, gaping mouths.

It's hard to believe because our kind has never taken females for granted. The idea that any race would treat their females like that is awful, unfathomable. Then again, we frequently take down slave ships, and many of those enslaved are females. We always hoped we would find a similar species to our own, but we never did, until now. And they are compatible, which we are all aware will change the course of history.

Our species was going to perish, but now we will be saved.

"How dare they? Those precious creatures being abused. I can't stand the idea of it." One board member says. His voice wobbles.

"We will protect them at all costs." Pipes in another. They all agree wholeheartedly, and I'm relieved. It seems everyone wants to help the females. They are our priority now.

"Do you have anything to tell us of Earth? Should we be prepared for danger?" Someone asks, and then everyone is looking at me. I shake my head, humans are weak, they pose no threat. Torint said that the females only pose a threat level 1. It's laughable how puny that is.

"Humans are low threat, very low threat, but they do have some weapons I have heard. There aren't many of them left. They have no societies. Their world was destroyed by wars and by famines. In most parts there are no dangerous predators."

We are well equipped to fight any creatures we come across. There are plenty of planets we've visited that have many strong beasts. We beat them every time.

"Good, very good. I still have one final question for you." A board member says, one who hasn't spoken the whole time.

I nod, inviting whatever he wants to ask.

"The female that won't leave your side, has she agreed to become your mate?" I can hear the excitement in his voice. One look at all of them, and

I know they are anxious to pair off each female to any worthy male. They want to repopulate Rytaria as quickly as possible, and it only makes sense.

We only had hope that something as miraculous as this could happen, and now it's here. Of course they would be waiting for more kits to be provided. The females are precious for more than their womb, of course they are, but their ability to provide life is essential.

I stare down at the ground, contemplating my answer. Torint informed me that kisses on the mouth lead to physically mating. The idea of my body joining with Penelope, and making a kit in the process, is more than tempting. She had never initiated it, and I don't know if it's because she is traumatized or if she is not impressed with me enough to make me her mate.

Her eyes never wander to others, she never acts as if she's displeased with my company, but I can't help but wonder if she wants someone stronger. Or, if she wants someone without a reputation.

"No, but I have hope that it will happen."

All of the members give me questioning looks, their eyes filled with disappointment. That is not the answer that they were expecting. I let out a gruff noise, annoyed that they assumed incorrectly in the first place.

"Well, if she doesn't show any interest, you should start introducing her to males to show her that she has many options. Many will want to join with her."

The words make me scowl. I hate the idea of Penelope being with another male. I clench my fists, hardening my jaw. I want to smash something at the image of it. I feel sick, furious, and... sorrow.

That can never happen. I won't let it. I'll have to wait for her to approach me as her mate. It is always a female's decision, I just have to sit aside patiently for her to decide.

Sorry that this is late, please forgive me, but yesterday was really hard. I will be very busy the next few weeks, so I will try my best to provide frequent chapters!

# |14|

**P**enelope

I think I might be in love. I never thought that I would ever fall in love. It seemed impossible after everything I've been through. But, people change. People change other people. Elik changed me.

It's all I can think about when I woke up today in a great mood. I follow him around as he does his daily duties. He goes to a meeting and let's me follow happily, holding my hand tightly in his as we walk down the long stretching corridors of the palace.

Even though it's beautiful here, I can't help but be a little jealous of Posy and Torint. They moved out to the countryside to continue their life together.

Torint gave up his life as a soldier to start a family with his mate. I find myself glancing up at Elik from time to time, wondering if he would do the same thing for me. I don't want to pressure him into anything. We haven't been together long, and I don't want to rush things if he's not comfortable with it.

I mean, why would he want to give up his career? Why would he want to give up living in this enormous palace? He would probably laugh in my face if I asked him to live in the middle of nowhere with me. He's a strong General, and his rank is noble. Why would he leave that behind for me?

As amazing as this place is, I don't know how long I want to be here. There are men literally everywhere that I look. I mean, it makes sense, it's a planet with only guys. That's why we're so special, I guess. I don't feel special, especially compared to someone like Jane. She went through the same crap I did, and she's happily eating up the attention of the Rytarians, and she's been spotted canoodling with the Emperor himself.

I wish I could be confident, but I'm becoming better every day. As long as I'm progressing, I should be proud of myself.

As we walk back to our apartment after a long day of running errands, I notice something strange going on. I grip Elik's hand a little tighter.

People that we pass stare at me, because of course they do, they never stop staring. They also stare at Elik. This stare is a different one, they seem to be suspicious. He even earns a few glares here and there, and I look back at each passerby with confusion. I glance up at Elik, and his facial expression remains passive, as if nothing is out of the ordinary.

He continues leading me until we're right back where we need to be. Hidden in the privacy of our own apartment from everyone else. Elik closes the door and moves to the bed, peeling back the covers for me.

It's sort of a routine of ours. He knows I like to lay down after a long day, he's only taking care of me. And yet, I don't slip into the comfy bed like I usually would. Instead, I put a hand on his arm and look up to him with concern.

"What is it, sweet one?" He's genuinely confused, and his words are so gentle but so heartbreaking.

"Why do people look at you like that, Elik? It's driving me crazy." I murmur, hating every single one of them. They're judgmental eyes and venomous glares. I've never been violent, but I felt like chasing them down and hurting them. Me of all people, as if my fist could even reach their faces.

Elik sighs, and presses his lips together. I have a feeling it has to do with his past. I told him he could tell me when he's ready, but curiosity is getting the best of me.

"If you still don't want to tell me, I understand. I just hate that you have to deal with this, that's all." I shrug, holding both of his hands and looking at his strong fingers.

He pulls me down with him onto the bed, forcing me into his lap as he smothers himself in my hair. I sit still for a moment, letting him collect himself as I wait patiently.

"I was only a small child when it happened. I have very few memories of my mother. I remember the sickness that took our females, and how everyone panicked as they started to die." He shakes his head, "My Mother was the last female alive. She was sick, and they tried to take her away."

I gasp, putting a hand to his chest to comfort him. I can't imagine how traumatic it was to live through that, especially as a little kid. Elik continues.

"She was in a lot of pain. My Pa was going mad because of it. Soldiers came to our home and dragged her away. He fought them, but they would not listen. They took her to the palace, and after a few weeks, they let us visit her."

I watch the tears form in his eyes. It's something I never thought I would see happen. Elik is so tough. I don't hold his tears against him. Men have emotions, they're allowed to cry too.

"They had all these tubes coming out of her, trying to keep her alive. She looked so frail, and had no life in her eyes. She smiled when she saw Pa, but then she started crying. She begged him to end her life, saying she could not take the pain anymore. She said they were trying to artificially impregnate her in hopes of making more females. It was cruel." Elik chokes on the words.

"My Pa told me to leave the room. When the doctors ran down the hall and the screams and shouts started, I knew he had fulfilled her wish. He killed her, out of love and mercy. She wouldn't have lived much longer, and it would've been so painful to keep her like that. He loved her too much to let her suffer."

I run a hand up and down his arm in hopes to comfort him. It just gets worse every time he opens his mouth. He somehow continues.

"They arrested my Pa. He was put to death, and I was sent to the academy to become a soldier. Ever since then, I've been cursed with the story of how my Pa brutality murdered my Mother because he didn't want anyone to have her, unless is was him. They're all lies. I was there that day, but not many believe me. They choose to hate me because it's my Pa's fault that the last female was killed. It is just the way things are." He sounds so resigned, like he doesn't really care. He's not even that upset about the way others treat him.

That's fine. I'll be angry enough for the both of us.

I wipe away his tears, and then mine, because I'm crying like a baby from hearing his story. We both have traumatic pasts, we both chose to stay silent. We are alike in so many ways.

"I'm so sorry. That's awful." Elik's dark eyebrows scrunch up in confusion.

"You did not do it. It isn't your fault." I feel like laughing at his innocent comment. He takes a lot of things too literally. It's cute.

"I hate that that had to happen. The universe sucks sometimes. You didn't deserve that, no one does. I don't care how they see you. You're perfect to me." I declare, and the grin that grows on his face, it's so worth it. It's hard for me to talk about how I feel, but Elik always makes me feel safe enough to speak my mind. He tucks a piece of hair behind my hair.

"Oh how you humble me little female. Thank you."

I answer by snuggling into his chest, content to stay here forever, but that's not possible. The world is always waiting, and I'm always procrastinating facing it.

Hope you enjoyed the chapter! Next one will be up on Wednesday. Love y'all

# |15|

## Elik

I slam the ball with my fist, watching it fly across the court as two males dive for it at the same time. They aren't so lucky. Their heads knock together, and Umner bursts into laughter.

Grinning slightly, I turn to Penelope who sits patiently on the side lines, legs swinging as she watches. She claps her hands in applause. She agreed to come along to our game, and I'm glad. I wouldn't have come if she didn't want to come with me. Not only would she be stressed being by herself, I would be worried the whole time she was out of my sight.

I'm glad she not only wants me for protection, but she also wants to spend time with me. It is a miracle to be lucky enough to be with her, let alone be the center of her attention.

"Rashin! Pay attention. We can win this." Ooli grumbles, rubbing his head as Umber continues to laugh and tease them. It's clear that the one called Rashin is embarrassed. He's one of Umner's friends, and he's just as young and dumb as my team member.

We are easily beating them. The large ball is tossed back and forth over the barrier where the other two males try to keep it from hitting the floor. We gain a point whenever the ball touches the other player's side.

It's not a very complicated game, and you can have many people playing as long as the number is even. But, it does get difficult when you are competitive, and the rest of the players are just as eager to be on the winning team.

Starting another round, we beat the ball back and forth a few times. It flies through the air easily before it hits Rashin right in the head. He yelps, slamming to the ground. His partner, Ooli, gets agitated very quickly.

"What do you think you are doing?" He demands, motioning to the ball that lay motionless on the ground. I wince, the poor kit, that ball is very heavy, it could not have felt good to be hit in the head with it.

Rashin shrugs, and then tilts his head, feeling it with his palm as he checks for injuries. I catch him looking off the court. I follow his eyes, finding myself very displeased with where he's looking.

"Stop that." I demand, and his brown eyes fall on me. I glare at him, taking a dangerous step forward in warning.

"Here we go again." Umner complains, rubbing an annoyed hand down his face as he watches.

"What? She is a female. She is beautiful, and I've never seen one before." He helps defensively. What he says is true, and I cannot deny that. Penelope is beautiful. She's absolutely perfect to be exact.

Of course I should not deny any male the right to gaze at a female when the majority of our race have never seen one before. It's unfair to say they cannot steal a glance. But, I can't control the overwhelming jealousy that fills me with it's vicious fire.

I don't want anyone to look at Penelope. I want to yell from the hill tops that she's mine, and mine alone. No male should look at her. No one should try to take her away from me.

"I don't want you looking at her."

Not only does it infuriate me in general, but Penelope is delicate. She is scared of males other than myself, and I don't want her to be frightened. She's so small, and our males are very large. It's no wonder she gets intimidated by our mere presence.

Rashin growls, taking a step towards me. Gone is his shy, youthful ways. He's been threatened, and he knows it, and he does not like it.

"You have no claim on her." He tells me, and I disagree.

"She's claimed me."

"Then why isn't she your mate?" Rashin counters, raising an eyebrow and glancing at Penelope. I follow his gaze once again.

The fragile human female has a pale, long neck, a neck that holds no claim mark on its soft flesh.

He has a point. I haven't claimed Penelope as my mate. It's my deepest wish, other than her happiness. Her joy is my priority, and I won't force my wishes on her if she doesn't happily agree.

It's why she doesn't already bear my mark to the world.

"She is there for the taking. Any male could take her from you. She's not yours. She could choose anyone, including me." He brags, and I have finally had enough of talking. I won't listen to another word.

I jump the barrier, all thoughts of fun and games leaving my mind as I land on him. I hear shouts from the other males, and a more feminine one as well. I leave it all behind when my body retaliates from the argument.

My fists fly in a blinding force of rage, each contact of my knuckles with Rashin's face aleives some of the fury that he's built up inside me. This is his fault. He took this on himself.

I growl when he struggles, and I feel someone grab my arm from behind. I wrench my elbow from the assaulting grip, continuing my search of pain.

Another attempt at pulling me away is made, and this time it's successful. I'm torn away, my arms being used as handle bars to get a grip on me, the two males using their combined strength to defeat my wrath. I snarl, wanting to get at Rashin but failing.

He hastily wipes the blood from his nose, his eyes wild as he glares at me. He opens his idiotic mouth to spew more hatred.

"Call the guards. Get him arrested. He deserves to be behind bars." He spits, and I find myself wondering why Umner would ever choose to be friends with him. He's a lunatic.

I hear a cry of outrage, a very delicate cry. I look back to see Penelope running over to where we stand. She stumbles, and I try to run to her to catch her, but I'm still being held firmly by Umner and Ooli.

The brave female steps between me and Rashin, and she's trembling from head to toe. I growl. He's terrified her, and so have I. She is traumatized enough already, and now I've shown her more violence and terror.

"No. Please. Please, don't take him away. Please." Her voice breaks at the same time as my heart. Umner loosens his hold, his mouth dropping open at the sweet but panicked words.

Penelope never speaks unless it's to me, and my friends are always shocked when it happens.

I use the opportunity to pull away, taking my precious female into my arms and picking her up. Her legs wrap around my waist, her arms winding around my neck. The poor thing clutches at me. She sniffles, and I know her well enough to know that she is trying to keep it together like the strong female that she is. She buries herself on my shoulder.

Rashin has the nerve to look sorry as the female shakes with silent sobs. I don't pay any attention to him, I simply carry her away, knowing she my one and true purpose.

Thanks for sticking with me! Hope you enjoyed the chapter. Don't be afraid to drop a vote and comment, it helps me out a lot

Next chapter will be on Wednesday. Love y'all so much. Stay home, stay safe, and wear your masks

# |16|

## Elik

I quickly take Penelope back to our small den where she will have peace and quiet. Thankfully, the small female has stopped her crying and has remained silent though our journey down countless hallways and corridors. Sometimes I curse this place. The palace is too large.

When we reach the den, I slam the doors shut behind us, separating us from the world of pain. Once I've set Penelope down, I tear off my shirt in frustration. I feel so hot from the inside out. Blood is splattered on my shirt, and stained on my knuckles.

I don't want Penelope to see the evidence of violence, so I flee to bathroom to wash it away before she can spot it. The sounds of the water running block everything out. It's all I can concentrate on while I scrub. I watch the pink water gurgle down the drain.

Once it's gone, I return to the main room with a heaving chest. I'm out of breath. I want nothing more than to go back and find that worthless piece of scum and make him cry like he did to my precious female. How dare him say those things?

I run a frustrated hand over my short hair, wishing I had something to punch. I need to take out this energy, this fury, and I want to take blood.

Penelope's soft hands prod at my arm, and I tear away from her, shielding my eyes from her. My pupils are likely dilated with brutality and darkness. She can't see that.

She's insistent though, and her touch is so different than the rough pulling I just experienced from the other males as they tore me away from my target. Penelope's hands are tiny and kind. I want them all over me.

I growl, annoyed that she won't quit. Can't she see that I am protecting her from myself? She wants what she wants when she wants it, but I can never be angry at her. She is far too perfect to be at fault.

"What is it, sweet human?" I ask her calmly, hiding the fury that's bubbling just under the surface. She's still pulling at me silently, and I sigh, turning to face her in a quick whirl that nearly knocks her over. I have to grab her slight shoulders to keep her from falling.

I'm reminded by how little Penelope really is. The top of her head doesn't even come to my shoulder, in fact, she barely makes it halfway up my arm. She's so delicate, I can hardly stand it. Knowing how vulnerable she is kills me.

What I see when I finally look into her eyes is kindness, but a heavy amount of fear as well. I'm so startled by it that I step back in horror. I knew it, I knew she would be afraid of me if she saw how volatile I look. If it weren't for that foolish Rashin, I wouldn't have made her feel scared.

"What happened back there?" She wonders softly, her voice a whisper in the quiet room.

"He was looking at you. It drove me mad." I explain in a short burst of words, unable to elaborate as heat climbs my spine at the reminder of what just happened only moments ago. It's still fresh.

Penelope looks away, staring at her short fingers with a twisted mouth as her eyes start leaking again. I hate the sight. When she cries, I feel absolutely powerless. I fall apart when she's upset.

"Don't cry, please don't be afraid. He's gone now, I won't let him near you." I promise, and I take her face in my hands. Her skin is so pale in comparison to mine, and there's a pretty pink splattered on her cheeks.

The female sniffles, a sound I would find adorable if it weren't for the emotion it shows. She can't be sad, I won't allow it, especially if I can do something about it.

"Why did he say those things?" Penelope presses, her lip trembling as she stares up at me through her wet eyelashes.

I raise an eyebrow, confused.

"What things?"

"Why.. why did he say I'm not your mate?" A little hiccup escapes her, and she stands firm despite her timid question. I'm astounded. I didn't expect her to ask that.

"Because you are not." I explain. She doesn't like my answer. Before I can grab her, she runs to the nest, burrowing herself in the pillows and blankets to hide herself from me. I head her sobs echo through the room, and I don't know what I'm supposed to do.

What is happening? I'm left feeling completely clueless. There's only one way to resolve this, and that's by taking with her.

Females are cute, but they are confusing.

I go to her side, sitting on the nest and grabbing her minuscule waist and pulling her out of the mess of sleeping material.

"What is wrong? Why do you continue to torture me with your tears?" I beg, touching Penelope's hair, and her face. She won't even look at me. She's angry with me, and I don't even know what I did. Is it because of my violent nature? Does she want a more calm male? A more timid partner?

"You said that we're not mates." She says, sorrow on her tongue, tears in her eyes.

I'm still confused. Penelope sighs.

"I thought we were." She clarifies, and then she shoves her face in a pillow with a groan. "I'm so stupid."

Her sobs start again, and I want them to cease, but I'm a little distracted. I'm stuck in my own mind, drowning in surprise and pure joy.

She wants to be my mate. All this time, she thought that we were already mates. I've never been so happy and confused at one time.

"Penelope." I say, and she ignores me. I want to be firm, but I'm too overjoyed. I'm also sad that my poor female is hurt. There is too much misunderstanding between us.

I grab her again, ripping her more forcefully away from her shelter of sorrow. I deposit her in my lap easily enough, my arms becoming a prison around her as she struggles to get away.

"You have not asked me to be your mate, but I will gladly accept your offer. I'm just afraid you will find me lacking." I admit, rocking her slightly to calm her nerves. I don't feel very steady, the mere idea of becoming her male is too tempting. I want her more than anything.

Penelope flails in my arms, I'm hardly affected by the action, but I loosen my hold regardless. Before I know it, my face is being yanked forward. Soft, plump lips push up against my own mouth.

I still, right before I go along with the activity. I kiss the sweet human back, loving the feel of her against me.

She starts becoming rougher, demanding more as her breath rushes in and out like a storm. I can't deny her anything. If she keeps going, I know where this road will end, and I don't have the self control to stop myself.

I push her away slightly, a difficult feat, not because of her strength, but because of the temptation Penelope poses. I have to remind myself that her brain is still injured, and she is still healing with time.

"We cannot, your past..."

"I want you. I know I got hurt in the past, but this time is different. I'm choosing this, that's what makes it different. I'm choosing you. I want you as my mate. You make me forget the past." She sighs, grabbing my hand and putting it over her heart. The organ thuds greedily under my palm.

My eyes flick up to hers in disbelief. She wants to mate. Right now. To join our bodies and become one, possibly creating a child in the process.

"You humble me, my human. I will treasure you."

Penelope giggles, I'm sure it is the most beautiful sound on the planet.

"I know, and I will treasure you." She becomes a little more serious. "Please, help me forget the past, and rebuild my future."

She smiles, pressing closer to me.

"Make me your mate."

And so, that is exactly what I do. I fall onto her in a mess of kissing and touching, and I have my way with her. A piece of my life shifts perfectly into place, and I know that I'm complete.

In case you haven't noticed.... I don't write smut Sorry! I'm too uncomfortable with it, and you'll have to forgive me since I posted this chapter early! Just felt like giving y'all a surprise during this crazy time of quarantine!

Next chapter will be up on WednesdayLove y'all!!!

## |17|

**Elik**

I wake up the next morning to a warm nest, and a naked female smooshed to my side. I waste no time, I flick on the light beside me, dimming it so it won't wake her. I stare down at my precious Penelope, remembering all we went through last night. I can't believe it was real. The mating, the marking. It was all real.

There's a fresh bite mark on her neck to prove it. I can't stop looking at her.

Her brown hair is tossed over the pillow in a mess. I pet the side of her face with the back of my hand, and she doesn't budge. Her breathing is even and slow. I wore her out completely. After one round of mating she passed out from exhaustion.

I chuckle under my breath, amused by that. She may be weak, but she has me trapped in her grasp, and I would do anything for her. The amount of power she holds over me is immense. I will make sure she is safe and happy no matter what the cost. I love Penelope more than anything else in the Universe.

Satisfaction is the next emotion to bubble up inside of me. She bears my mark, she bears my scent between her legs. Everyone will know who she belongs to. Everyone will know we are mates. They have to respect that. Penelope is taken.

A ring echoes through the room, a new message being received, I turn quickly to my slumbering mate. Her lips twitch, but she doesn't move. She's so cozy and warm under her covers, she doesn't care a thing about what's happening in the outside world.

I press a soft kiss to her cheek, silently thanking her for the gifts she's disposed on me. I say a silent prayer that my kit already grows in her womb.

Shifting the blanket off of myself, and then settling it back down, I cross the room naked as the day I was born. The electronic pad by the door lights up under my fingers, a message flashing across the screen. I swipe down, reading the alert that was so important to disturb me. It better be worth dragging me out of bed with my mate.

I love that word. Mate. I could say it all day long and never tire of it.

The message is from Umner. He wants to talk about what happened yesterday, and discuss what we need to do to diffuse the situation with Rashin. I moan in annoyance. Obviously this was coming, but I wanted to delay it as long as possible.

The desire to just stay in my nest with my mate is great, but I have to face this so it can be over and done with. I'll have nothing to regret or fear, we can simply head forward into the future together.

I dress quickly in my uniform, not too thrilled to be putting clothing back on after all that transpired last night.

I take a glance back at Penelope, savoring the view of her with a smile before slipping out the door, hoping to return before she wakes. I travel down the hallways quickly, the coordinates for where we will meet already memorized from the years I've spent in the Emperor's palace.

Not many people are out this time of morning, it's too early for there to be much action in the corridor. I walk as fast as my legs will take me without running. I don't know why Umner summoned me so soon after waking. It seems an odd thing, but I do not question it.

Umner is my friend, and he wants to help me.

I enter the room he told me to come to, and I look around. It's dark and dusty in the room. I've never been to this room before, so I'm shocked that even Umner knows where it is.

I get a bad sensation in my stomach, a sinking feeling. I back away, ready to bolt, when someone grabs me from behind. I yell out to anyone that will hear me, praying for help as I'm pushed to the ground mercilessly.

There is no hope as a knee presses into my back, the bone digging into my spine. It's uncomfortable, and I wriggle. I cannot escape, the weight is too heavy.

A light flickers on, and it reveals several males.

"So, you fell for that, did you?" Rashin steps into the beam, and I snarl. I should have known he was behind this. He smiles smugly.

"You tricked me!" I'm outraged. He used my own friend's name against me, coaxing me out of the safe haven I've built for myself and Penelope.

"And so what? You think you deserve a mate? A female? After what your Pa did?" He shakes his head as he mocks me. The few other males in the room stand around at Rashin's sides, and it's clear that they agree with what he has to say. They glare at me with hatred, with suspicion. I hate those looks, I've been dealing with them my whole life.

Rashin gets closer, going onto one knee and taking a whiff of me. An expression of clear disgust crosses his young face.

"It would seem like you took care of making her your mate. I only encouraged you after all. Well, it's too bad, because you won't be seeing her again." He tells me, spitting the words out one at a time. I glare at him in reply.

I won't be taken from my mate, I can't allow that. I'll do anything to get free and get back to her side.

Rashin looks up, addressing the male on my back.

"Take him to the dungeons. No one ever goes down there, they won't suspect a thing." I'm being hoisted up in the air, dragged away as the foolish young male yells out on more command.

"And go grab the human female. We need to bring her to the Emporor. He will decide what is to be done to her." I yell out, ripping myself away from the strong grip of the male behind me and running for Rashin.

I can't let this happen. My mate, my sweet little female, she will be terrified without me. She won't be able to handle unfamiliar males taking her from her nest.

Right before I can reach him and his shocked face, I'm thrown to the ground, my head bouncing on the hard floor. My vision swims, and right before I fall into the dark, I hear more haunting words to chase me into my nightmares.

"Who knows? Maybe our Emperor will reward me with giving her to me as a mate. After all, I did take down a dangerous criminal. She will be begging for me to mate her. Just you wait and see."

|18|

P enelope

 I yawn, and stretch, feeling like a well rested cat as my limbs extend. A satisfied smile splays on my face when I remember what happened. Oh my gosh, I can't even believe it.

Elik and I did it, and I don't know how to process it. After all that's happened to me, I feel like I need to be confused, or that I need to over analyze it. I realize that I'm just so happy, so why do I need to question that?

When I look around, expecting to see my mate, I'm met with an empty room. I don't have long to be confused before there's furious pounding at the front door. I nearly jump out of my skin at the noise.

There's yelling, but no sensical words that cant be desiphered theough the thick metal door. Fear spikes through me. I leap out of bed, trying to make a dash for the bathroom, when I suddenly realize that I'm naked.

My face flushes with heat, and I glance at the noisy door. I quickly grab some clothes, not looking or caring what they are. I find out that the shirt is way too big for me, it hits my knees. It's because this is Elik's shirt. I would know that smell anywhere, it's imprinted in my brain.

I don't have any time to hide, the door slides open. I take a few hurried steps backwards at the sight of 3 big, burly Rytarian males. They stare at me for a mere few seconds, then they descend on me.

Panic stirs me into action. I side step them, circling them with wide eyes. I want to cry, but I can't seem to get any tears going. Anger is all I find, and some fear.

"Female. You must come with us." One commands me, glaring at me since I dared to dodge him.

I open my mouth, willing words to come out. After all the effort, nothing happens. I close my mouth in disappointment. Elik still remains the only one I can talk to.

"Come on. We don't have a lot of time." He growls impatiently, grabbing for my shirt, I slap his hand away and walk towards the door skittishly. I wonder where Elik has disappeared to, and why he would leave me. I'm sure it was for something important. He would never abandon me.

The males exchange glances, and one pipes in.

"We will take you to your mate." I perk up at those wonderful words, wanting more than anything to be returned to him. I eye them angrily. Why did they have to just burst into my room? I have no idea what's going on here, but I don't like it.

I'm not sure they're telling the truth, but I'm sure that something fishy is going on here. I don't know what to do. For one thing, I have major issues trusting men, and on the other hand, I know that Rytarian males are inherently trustworthy. They worship females. Maybe I'm just being paranoid.

I nod my head, agreeing and hoping I'm making the right choice. This place is huge, I don't know what I'll do if I get lost. I'll just have to trust them to lead the way.

They walk out of the room, allowing me to follow them down the hallway. I wrap my arms around myself for comfort, I'm surrounded on all sides by unfamiliar testosterone and I can't stand it. I think of Elik's warm body and feel a little bit better. The only sound through the hallways is our steps, and their's are a little more sure footed than mine.

I'm quiet the whole time, and so are they, because there's nothing to say.

I can feel my heart beating in my throat, like a warning.

Once we get down another long corridor, a new male appears out of a door, practically falling out of the room. He stares at me, a grin spreading over his face.

"She came willingly? Elik said she wouldn't be happy when she found out he was in prison." He remarks, his tone colored in surprised confusion. I can feel the blood drain from my face as his words dawn on me.

Before I can try to bolt, strong hands clamp onto my arms, and I struggle against them. A sound of desperation leaves me. I'm afraid, terrified as they drag me away. My legs drop, and I'm yanked around like a rag doll as they haul me up by the elbows. They won't let go.

I scream, absolutely outraged. They easily overpower me, and I try not to panic completely. Tears fill my eyes. I just want my mate.

Did they hurt him? Why is he in prison? Worry floods my system, and I tremble, knowing that there are too many unanswered questions, and that I'm completely at these men's mercy.

"Elik! Help me!"

Elik

My mate's cries for help have me fighting a complete breakdown. I grip the bars of my cage, the small cell barely able to contain me and all of my rage.

The male guarding me smirks down at me, holding his weapon tightly to his chest. His blaster is fully loaded, but he doesn't seem very capable of using it well. He's young, much like the other males that conspired against me.

"You were foolish to think a female would want you." He tells me, and I glare, shaking with held in anger. I want to tear limbs apart, make blood spill. What these males are doing is blasphemy. Separating mates is not right. Frightening females is not right, and if they hurt her in the slightest I won't hesitate to kill them all.

"Why are you doing this?" I snarl, and his face grows serious.

"That female deserves a worthy male, all of us are hoping she will pick one of us. I'd give anything to have a female." He says, and the words are maddening. I want to hurt him.

He isn't completely gone mad, he's just a misled youth. Rashin is the true evil one. It is rare for Rytarians to become corrupt, it's why our jail cells are often empty. But this male, his mind has been twisted by his friend. There is only one thing I can do to rid the world of Rashin's evil, and I look forward to it. But first, I need to free myself from my cage.

"Do you want to know what it feels like to mate with a female?" I ask, and the words taste like poison in my mouth. I disgust myself, but I need him closer.

His eyes grow wide with desire, and the poor kit moves in to get the information. Once his gun is lowered, I grab the front of his shirt and pull him forward until his head slams into the prison bars. He's immediately knocked out, and I lower his limp body to the floor silently.

"I cannot be separated from my mate." I growl, reaching for the key hanging from his fingers, and pulling them out. I immediately go to work unlocking the door to free myself.

When the door swings open, I flee, going for the hallway to where the sound of my mate's fear came from. I can't stop picturing my poor, sweet Penelope. She's probably terrified. Those males will pay for what they've done, as soon as I can get my hands on them.

It's no time before I spot Rashin, I try to run the other direction, desperate to get away from him before he sees me. His group of misfits are likely close by, ready to take me down.

I sprint, but when I turn a corner I literally run into another male. It takes moments to realize that he's one of Rashin's friends, and he tries to grab me. I dodge the younger male, determined to get to the Emperor so I can save my mate. I am fueled by pure love that bursts through my veins.

Finding Penelope and protecting her is my priority.

"Get him!" Someone yells, likely Rashin, and I pick up the pace, pouring on the speed as my legs pump harder. But, it's all in vain.

I'm surrounded, there are too many of them, and I am gripped by despair as fingers take me into hand. They have me imprisoned in their hold. Rashin is in front of me, looking pleased. He nods his head happily.

"Let's go pay the Emperor a visit, shall we?" He asks, and I sag in relief. This male has no idea my connection to the Emperor. He is in for a surprise.

Even as they drag me away, I try to calm my racing heart.

Hold on, my mate, I am coming for you. You won't have to wait long, because I would fight to the death to be by your side.

# |19|

## Penelope

I'm surprised when the abusive males finally stop. I lift my head, trying to figure out where I am. There's lots of windows and tapestries and paintings. The room is huge with a super tall ceiling that goes on forever. I blink away the bright light as my eyes adjust.

I stare. Despite my predicament, I can't help the curiosity that builds over the obviously ancient castle. This is a room built for a King, or an Emperor.

My head snaps up at my name being called, and I'm shocked to see Jane running towards me with open arms.

"Let her go! Oh my gosh. Penelope, are you alright?"

She scoops me up into her arms, and I give a cry as sobs attack me. I can't breathe. I hear her yelling at the guards that had me, telling them to get lost. I let her lead me away while she continues to rage protectively. I haven't seen her in a week or two, but it feels like forever.

When I open my eyes again, she's looking at someone behind me. I blink away the tears, overwhelmed by how fast everything is happening. I want my mate. I need him.

"What is going on here?!" A booming voice demands, and my head snaps up to the Emperor. I've only seen him once, but he isn't someone I would forget. He's very handsome, his features unlike so many of the other Rytarian males I've seen. His face is made up of sharp planes, and right now they're twisted into a sneer.

Jane continues to fuss over me like a mother hen. I look back up at what's going on, and the Emporor is storming up to the males with so much anger in his step that I think he might hurt them. His guards come forward to get into position, prepared to protect their leader at all costs.

"We were just following Rashin's orders! He told us that the female needed to be saved, but that she would resist us." One explains, glancing nervously back and forth. I don't have any sympathy for him, and I wonder if that makes me a bad person.

"And you really didn't think to question why this female wouldn't come willingly?" The Emperor demands. He runs a frustrated hand down his face. "Why would you believe this Rashin? What did the male tell you?"

The question stuns them. The sight of them still standing there makes me want to cry harder, but I can only think of Elik. They said he was in prison. He couldn't have possibly done something so wrong to end up there. My heart aches for him, and I want to hurt these people for wronging him. I've never had a violent inkling in my life.

"He said that Elik would hurt her." He shrugs, and the other one looks just as bashful. The Emporor opens his mouth to speak, but is silenced when the doors to the throne room open again.

I sniffle, looking at the new arrivals, and then I wrench myself free when I see my mate among them. His face is towards the ground, his enormous figure slouched as he's carried through the doors.

I almost get to him when someone grabs me. It's one of the Emperor's guards, stopping me from reaching my mate as he's held hostage.

I sob, fighting with every ounce of strength I have left.

"Elik! No! Let me go!" I scream, so angry and so determined that I don't even think about speaking. I have to say something.

"What is the meaning of this? Are you Rashin?" The Emperor demands, and Rashin steps forward gladly, a gleeful look painted across his stupid face. I only glance at him for a second before I look back to my mate.

Elik looks up at me in quiet determination. His eyes are so intimate. He wants to be by my side, just as much I need him. I long to be with him, but it seems the world is against us.

"They became mates, and we all know what happened with his Pa. He killed his own mate. Are we going to sit by and let that happen again?" He asks, motioning to Elik like he's no more than a beast.

Tears run down my face, but they're not tears of fear, they are tears of sorrow. They are tears of anger. How dare they? How dare someone treat my mate like this?

"No!" I yell, trying to tear myself free and failing. Elik's eyes grow wide, everyone turns to face me in surprise. The Emperor lifts a hand, and his guard immediately lets me go.

I make a break for it, but Elik yells out too.

"No, my sweet mate. Do not come closer. I don't want these males to hurt you." He demands, so I stop, but I can't stop the sob that wracks my chest. My skin prickles, my throat is clogged, but I still want to speak.

"Let him go. He's innocent." I plead, but they don't listen to me, they all look to their leader.

The Emperor looks back and forth between us, obviously aware of what's happening here. He puts his fingers out, and Jane goes to him, putting her much smaller hand in his. They stand together, and it's now that I realize that they are together. Are they mates?

There's a light of admiration in his eyes when he stares down at my friend. I already know the answer. He loves her.

"I have a question for you, Rashin." The Emperor murmurs, and the young Rytarian steps forward with an air of arrogance.

"Yes, your majesty?"

The Emperor's head turns.

"Did you think to ask the female what she thinks of Elik?" He wonders, and Rashin's eyebrows furrow as if he never thought of such a thing. I stare at Elik, now understanding why he seems so calm despite everything happening. He trusts his ruler, his Emperor. Elik knows that everything will be okay.

"No, your majesty, I did not ask her." Rashin admits, rubbing a hand across the back of his head. He seems embarrassed actually. He looks at me with curiousity. He's looked at me before, like at the volleyball game, but this time is different. He's hoping I'll support his claim that my man is abusive. There's a question in his eyes, he's hoping I'll stand with him.

Little does he know that I have something else in mind.

"He's not a monster! Elik is my mate. The holder of my heart. He's a protector. He's my protector." I say, loud and clear, more confident in my voice than I've ever been, even before I went through my imprisonment. I glance at my mate, my perfect companion, and I see a rare smile on his face.

I can tell from that single look that I've made him proud.

The males holding Elik captive appear shocked, like they don't know what to do. Instead of following Rashin's orders, they look to the Emperor, who nods his head once.

"You heard the female. Release her mate. He is an honorable male, and he does not deserve to be treated like a criminal."

They immediately release Elik, and he falls to the ground on his knees. I run to him, finally able to throw myself in his arms. His face goes to my neck, and his strong fingers cling to my back as he pulls me into him. He's still on his knees, and we're the same height now, on the same level.

I try to pull away, but he won't let me go. It hasn't been long since we were separated, but it feels like an eternity. He's been just as affected by this as me.

Elik finally lets me lean back, but his arms remain firm. I take his handsome, rugged face in my hands, and stare into his electric eyes. He stares at me as I run my fingers through his beard, pretending like we're the only people in the room. A sheen of moisture covers his gaze.

"I've missed you, my mate." He whispers, and I nod my head in agreement. I couldn't say it better myself.

"I love you. Don't ever leave me." I plead, and he sighs, not missing a beat.

"Never of my free will. I love you." He assures me, proceeding to hold me tight like nothing in the world can hurt us anymore, and maybe nothing else ever will. Maybe we've lived through all the hard times and everything will go up from here.

Even if that's not the case, even if we did have a rocky road ahead of us, I know we can get through it, just as long as we're together.

# |20|

## Elik

Not long after the incident at the palace, everything changed quickly.

I demanded justice from the Emperor, and he wholeheartedly agreed to have the issue resolved. Rashin was imprisoned after what he did, and is awaiting his trial in a jail cell. I hope his punishment will fit his crime. He terrified my poor mate, harassed me, and he is going to pay for it. Unfortunately, I won't stick around to see what becomes of the young warrior because I'm taking Penelope away from here.

As soon as I could get back to our den, I called Torint and asked him exactly how much land he had and if he minded us moving out there the very next day. Living in the middle of nowhere sounded great after what happened. Thepalace failed us, the thick walls anything but protective.

Neither of us had much to pack, and I'm thankful. We worked quickly to put everything in a bag and get a ride to where Torint has settled with his human mate.

Penelope and I ended up on a travel cruiser, the pilot was already heading in that direction and agreed to take us along. Thankfully, I had permission from the Emperor to take my female away from the palace. I was nervous that I would be denied, there are only 3 females on our planet, and I was pleasantly surprised that I was granted permission to take mine away.

The Emperor kindly informed me that him and Jane had become mates. I'm very happy for him, and I was glad that he understands the need to protect them at all costs. Leaving is what's best for my precious Penelope.

When we arrive at Torint and Posy's little farm, I'm surprised by the sight of the pregnant human female standing on the front porch waiting for us to arrive. Her belly has grown significantly to a swell, and she holds the bump with pride as she beams down at us.

I look around for Torint, even as I hold my mate tightly to my side. He's nowhere in sight, and I wonder why. He doesn't seem like the type to leave his mate alone for long, especially when she's carrying his kit.

"Come on in, I'll show you to your room." Posy says, waving an arm as we follow her into her den. The poor female practically waddles with effort.

I look down at my own female, wondering what she will look like swollen with our offspring growing in her womb. I yearn for it, excited at the idea of being a Pa, if not a little frightened. It will be a large responsibility, but I will try my hardest. I want a family with Penelope more than anything.

"Torint will be in soon. He has a surprise for you." Posy tells us on a sigh, catching her breath. The room she guides us to is small, but big enough for now. The bed is spacious, the closet acceptable.

I perk up at her mention of her male. I wonder what he has in store for us.

"I'm so happy y'all are here!" The human squeals, grabbing my mate's arm and pulling on it in excitement. If she were a male, I would hit her for the offense. But, they are females. They cannot possibly be in danger in each other's company. "I've been bored out of my mind! Torint barely lets me out of the house."

Penelope smiles kindly, not showing too much emotion, but I can tell she's happy to have a friend other than myself. I'm glad she is being more social, even if she won't say a word.

Except for when I was imprisoned, then she suddenly had courage to speak her mind. I was humbled by my mate's loving words. She called me her protector, and I will gladly accept the title with honor. I will do anything for her.

"Let's go find Torint, he's taking longer than I thought he would." Posy says, and she leads Penelope away again, hardly giving me time to put our luggage on the nest before they disappear out the door. I follow with an amused grumble.

Females. I will never fully understand them.

We walk through the home, and it's cozy. It's not overly large, but not too tiny either. It's not as big as the den Posy had on earth, but I still enjoy it. Females always have an instinct to make a den their own, there are pillows and flowers, things I have no clue about. And the strong walls and ceilings were obviously built to accommodate a Rytarian's bulk.

"Honey, they're here!" Posy yells as she goes out the back door, carefully taking each step. When we follow her outside, I spot Torint walking in the grass.

He wears no shirt, and his tan skin is licked in sweat that glints under the sun. He holds a long log of wood on his shoulders, proceeding to drop it on the ground with a thump when he spots us. It's clear the male has been working hard.

When his mate reaches his side, he puts a hand on her swollen waist, tugging her towards him gently so he can bend to give her a kiss on her head. He has to bend quite far, it only reminds me of my own mate. Humans are tiny things.

"I made some drinks. I'll go get them, you need to stay hydrated." She insists, slapping his chest to dislodge him. Her male lets her go reluctantly. She heads back to the den while Torint grins, watching her bottom while she walks with hungry eyes.

I snort. The male has always been a warrior, but he is different with his female. But so am I, I have never felt so defenseless as when I'm with my Penelope. I want her all the time.

I put an arm over her tiny shoulders, pulling her right to my side.

"Come, I'll show you what I'm working on." He says, motioning with a hand as he picks the log back up, walking away. We follow, and I watch the excitement grow on my mate's face.

It takes a while, but I see where we're going. A large stack of wood logs, and a rock platform poured into the ground. If I didn't know any better, I would say Torint is building a den. I can only guess it's for my mate and I to share.

"I hope it is a good size, and that you like the location." He says, looking around at the sparse trees. It's quite a flat part of the planet, this farming valley, but it is still very beautiful. The sun shines hot in this area, which makes it perfect for large foods to grow. Most parts of Rytaria get a lot of rain, but not the farming valley.

"It's perfect, thank you." Penelope whispers, her words so quiet you can barely even hear her, but Torint does. He raises his eyebrows, but smiles.

"You are very welcome." We're both surprised with the sentence she granted him. Penelope is constantly progressing, and I'm so proud of her. I didn't expect her to be doing so well.

I jump when I feel something soft sneak between my ankles, looking down to see an orange ball of fluff with pointed ears. It's Posy's cat, Weasly, a creature from Earth. He looks up at me and makes a rumbling sound.

"What do you want, little creature?" I ask, and Penelope laughs, wiggling out of my grip to bend and pick up the pet. She scratches him behind the ear, and cuddles him close to her chest.

"It means he likes you." She informs me, and I can't look away from her sweet nature. She has a maternal instinct already. I wonder if her body has already accepted my seed. I wouldn't be surprised, because she has let me mate her many, many times, almost every night. She thoroughly enjoys our coupling.

"Y'all want drinks?" Posy calls, walking up with a tray in hand, covered in glasses of juice. Torint growls low.

"You should not be walking this far by yourself, my mate." He scolds her, and she rolls her eyes at him, handing him a drink.

So, we all stand and drink, enjoying each other's company as we laugh and dream of the future. I can't keep my hungry hands off my mate, wondering when we'll finally get alone time so I can show her just how much I love her, because I can't wait much longer.

# epilogue

A few months later

Penelope waited patiently on the back porch, wondering where her mate was as she held the perfect bundle of joy in her arms. She bounced up and down, soothing the child with ease.

The more she stared down at the beautiful baby girl, the more Penelope wished that she had a baby of her own.

After a few weeks of hearing about all the crying that had been keeping poor Posy wide awake, she thought she could stand to wait years to have her own child. However, with the precious infant in her arms, she knew instantly that she wanted a baby more than anything.

The precious thing started up at her with hazy eyes, not quite able to focus yet with her green irises. Her thick black hair was gifted from her father, and her pale skin from her mother. Hazel was a perfect mix of her parents.

She lifted a pudgy hand, shoving it in her mouth impatiently as she suckled on her fingers. Penelope giggled, knowing that it meant the child was hungry for her Mother's milk.

Even though she didn't want to wake Posy from her much needed nap, she had to bring Hazel back before she started to fuss over her hunger.

Penelope made herself known with a gentle knock on the door to Posy's bedroom.

"Come in." Called a groggy voice through the wood, so Penelope opened the door and made her way to the sleepy new Mother.

"Someone's hungry. Sorry to wake you." Penelope said softly, her voice still gaining confidence with each use of her vocal chords.

Posy waved a hand in playful dismissal.

"I'm not surprised, don't worry about it. I got a few hours of sleep in. I'll be fine." She reached out her arms for her child, and Penelope obliged. "Come here, princess. Mommy missed you."

Posy nuzzled her baby's little face, giving her a few kisses before undoing her shirt, preparing to feed her. Hazel started rooting around for a nipple, Greedy for her meal.

Penelope looked away, not wanting to intrude on the private moment. She said her goodbyes to Posy and Hazel before leaving the house, impatient to get to her own family.

Her family of 2 that is, it was still just her and Elik in their home, but she didn't mind. She loved her mate with all her heart, even if there wasn't a child for them to spoil quite yet.

It wasn't for lack of effort, but there was still no sign of a baby. After a few doctor's visits, they were told that everything is in order, it's just taking a little bit of time. The delay could very well be attributed to the stress that Penelope had been under for the last few months. It wasn't surprising, and as soon as they heard it from the doctor, Elik was always trying to make her more relaxed.

Messages and baths were a daily necessity in his book, as well as lots of love making.

It was obvious to Penelope that Elik wanted a "kit" as he called them. When he first saw Hazel, he fell in love, almost immediately demanding that they have one of their own.

Penelope agreed, all too willing to have a baby to cuddle and nurture.

The sound of conversation drew her, and she glanced up to see the two Rytarians walking towards the house after being in the fields harvesting the crops.

They made it work, living out here, making a living off of the land and the various other resources they got from the farm animals. Animals that Penelope still couldn't get over. They were very strange looking, one species was a pig sort of creature, except it had a trunk.

She ran down to meet her man, throwing herself into his arms. Elik didn't hesitate before picking her up and planting a long kiss on her lips.

Torint simply laughed, saying goodnight before hurrying into the house to see his mate and baby. He did that every night, always excited to see them again after a few hours of work.

"How was your day?" Penelope asked, leaning back in his strong arms to get a glimpse of his handsome face. Elik grinned, her favorite expression in the world.

"Better now, of course. I thought of you the whole time." He replied, and Penelope has it in her mind to tease him.

"I didn't think of you one bit." She said cheekily, and Elik narrowed his eyes in playful suspicion. "Instead I thought of all the babies you'll give me."

Elik's eyes lit up, always thrilled at the mention of kits with his mate.

"Well, I guess we better go to our den, shouldn't we?" He asked, already walking away with the love of his life in his arms. She laughed hard, gripping him around the neck to steady herself. She couldn't stop the smile that stretched her cheeks.

Penelope never knew she could be this happy after all she had to live through. She realized that being into that cage, she was living for something, waiting patiently for a certain someone to come along. She lived for her mate, even then, and she would continue to live for him for the rest of her life.

"I guess we should. You better hurry before I change my mind." She teased.

And with that, Elik sprinted.

www.ingramcontent.com/pod-product-compliance
Lightning Source LLC
Chambersburg PA
CBHW072213070526
44585CB00015B/1315